great interview

G R E A T interview

Successful Strategies for Getting Hired

by Vivian V. Eyre

with Diane Osen and Jennifer Williams

Library of Congress Cataloging-in-Publication Data
Eyre, Vivian.
    Great interview : successful strategies for
getting hired / by Vivian Eyre, Diane Osen,
and Jennifer Williams.—1st ed.
        p. cm.
    Includes bibliographical references.
    ISBN 1-57685-304-7 (pbk.)
    1. Employment interviewing   I. Osen, Diane, 1956-
II. Williams, Jennifer, 1955- III. Title.

HF5549.5.I6 E96 2000
650.14—dc21

                                        00-030158

Printed in the United States of America

9 8 7 6 5 4 3 2 1

First Edition

ISBN 1-57685-304-7

For Further Information
For information on LearningExpress, other LearningExpress products,
or bulk sales, please write to us at:

LearningExpress
900 Broadway
Suite 604
New York, NY 10003

www.LearnX.com

CONTENTS

great interview

INTRODUCTION

YOU CAN LEARN from anything—whether buying tickets to a concert or talking to a neighbor. You simply have to see the interaction as a learning experience in order to walk away with fresh ideas and wisdom.

Going though the interview process is going to be one of the best learning experiences of your life. It is your right of passage into a world of meaningful work, financial independence, and contribution to society. And it all starts with a great interview—because this interview can lead to you landing the job of your dreams. It's true that some people say that interviewing is just a necessary evil, an exercise that saps time and energy. But they are mistaken. As a career coach, educator, and former corporate executive I have a unique perspective. I have interviewed candidates for countless positions, coached interview candidates, and had my own interview experiences. I feel strongly that interviewing is one of the best learning experiences you'll have in your career.

Interviewing will tell you a lot about yourself. It will tell you if you have the discipline to prepare for an important event. Because interviewing is high stakes for the candidate, it involves a certain amount of pressure. You'll find out how you communicate and relate to others in a stressful situation. The more interviews you go on, the more likely you'll be to land a job—but there's bound to be rejection along the way. You'll need to be resilient and bounce back after you hear "No thank you," and then motivate yourself to keep at it the next day. You'll also find out how good you are at overcoming obstacles and persevering in the face of them. It's as if you are training for an athletic event.

Besides learning about yourself, you'll practice business skills that you'll need to use throughout your career, such as gaining visibility, networking, persuading, and building rapport with different types of people. The more you learn about how others think, their unique perspectives, and what they value, the more well rounded you'll become as a person. These opportunities for increased self-awareness and business skills translate to vital life lessons that you'll rely on whether at work, with your family, or in your community.

Think about interviewing as your doctoral program. There will be no grades, and your dissertation will be having a great interview. If you do, you'll graduate by landing a job. The good news is that finding a job uses some of the skills you already used to pass challenging courses in college. It's a process—small challenging steps to be mastered over time. But there are different rules for having a great interview. And that's what this book will help you master.

Many people have contributed to making this book the best, most up-to-date resource on interviewing for college students and college graduates. A special thanks to Amanda Leff, Margaret Piskitel, Sandy Gade, Maggie Dunsmuir, Jennifer Farthing, Elisabeth

Starkman, and Lisa Laudico for their excellent writing, researching and networking skills—they prove that the methods described in this book really work.

We wish you every success in your job search.

C H A P T E R 1

getting started

Gathering Your Resources,
Networking, and Embarking on Your Job Search

IT SHOULD COME to you as a tremendous relief to learn that looking for a job doesn't need to be a daunting proposition. In fact, the process can be exciting and fulfilling. And, ultimately, it is a process *you can control*. Many of the skills and disciplines that you learned in college, and that served you so well as a student, will come into play when you start looking for a job. In other words, you should feel confident not only that you are equipped to find the job you want, but that the process itself will be an enlightening and memorable one.

The most important step in the job-search process, of course, is to land an interview. But for many recent graduates, this step is the hardest. One of the biggest obstacles is the erroneous belief that getting an interview is a matter of chance. In fact, the process of getting an interview is more like solving a statistics problem than it is a matter of luck: the more resumes you send out, the more likely you are to get an interview. It's as straightforward as that. It also means that the more resources you use, the better your chances will be of getting an interview for the job you want.

The process that leads to a job interview may actually start with an interview: an informational interview that you conduct to gather information from a human resources manager, recruiter, or a network contact. Informational interviews are discussed in Chapter 5 (see p. 106).

WHAT *ARE* YOUR RESOURCES?

Before you begin to map out your strategy to find a job, you need to consider the resources that are available to you:

- What are they?
- How can they be best utilized or accessed?
- Which ones will bring you the highest degree of success in landing an interview?

Newspaper Advertisements

Most people begin their search with a careful look through the advertisements in the Help Wanted section of a newspaper. This is one of the easiest and most useful ways of researching interview possibilities. However, want ads can be misleading. In the career world, the best jobs often don't reach newspapers, which means that you get a limited sense of the jobs that are available. Also, since employers are conscious of the cost of advertising, they tend to put only bare bones information in their ads. To get more information, you may want to call about a position before applying: human resources personnel or another company representative should be able to give you detailed information on the nature of the job and the necessary qualifications. If the ad was placed by a recruiting firm, call the recruiter before you apply; she will give you more information about the job and help you highlight key skills and abilities in your cover letter. By researching advertised positions ahead of time, you'll be able to eliminate jobs that are not suited to your needs.

Better yet, try to talk to someone who already works for the company you are interested in. Your college career center may be able to give you the name of a recent graduate who has gone to work for the company, particularly if the firm recruits on campus. You might also consider calling a firm's human resources department; they may be able to tell you more about a particular position or put you in touch with someone working in that department. You may also be surprised to find that you already have a connection to the firm. This is where your network of peers, or people you know who are already in the working world, comes in handy. Ask your parents, friends, relatives, and peers if they know anyone who can tell you more about a certain company or field (more information on networking will be presented later in this chapter and in Chapter 2). You will enhance your chances of making the right choice about a company and presenting your credentials most effectively if you talk to someone who already works there.

Career Centers

By the time most college or university students have reached their junior year they are familiar with the career center on campus, where they can either access information about jobs from a database or receive guidance from a career counselor. However, information about the kinds of jobs that are available is sometimes limited by the relationship between a college or university and certain employers. For example, some schools are known for a certain specialty, such as placing their graduates in non-profit organizations or in financial services. Consequently, they tend to attract employers mostly from those areas. The key here is to understand your career center's objectives. With whom do they have relationships? If you are not interested in any of the employers that come to your campus, you will need to investigate other options.

Even if your career center does not focus on the industries that interest you the most, it may still be a useful resource. Most career centers have resource centers or small libraries in which you can find brochures, contact lists, annual reports, and other information. Your career center should have information about public sector jobs, such as the FBI or other government positions, and may have industry-specific information, such as a list of all the law firms in a particular state. Career centers may also conduct resume or cover letter workshops. Finally, career counselors should be on hand to give you advice on finding jobs and preparing for interviews.

Another on-campus resource is your school's alumni office. Often, this department keeps a list of alumni and their current careers. It's worth the effort to go through this list. If an alumna works for a company that interests you, you may have found a key person to put in your network. Networking will be discussed, in detail, later in this chapter.

Recruiting firms

The best thing about recruiting firms is that they advertise jobs that are actually open. And they are highly motivated. Recruiting firms earn their income from the placements they make. Therefore, they are very eager to find the right person for a job. The downside is that recruiting firms generally like to make placements happen as quickly as possible, because more placements mean more revenues for the firm. It's more expedient for recruiters to match round pegs with round holes—people who have the exact experience listed in the job description in front of them. If your employment experiences are not an exact match for the positions available, you may have difficulties using a recruiting firm.

For instance, suppose you and your friend, Amy, are both interested in an administrative position at a small public relations firm. You ran a summer camp for children out of your backyard, while Amy spent her summer working as an administrative assistant at a large law firm. Even though the two of you may have developed similar organizational and interpersonal skills, Amy will be a more appealing job candidate to a recruiter, simply because Amy's office experiences will be perceived as a closer match for a job calling for "at least three months administrative experience."

The bottom line is: *do* investigate recruiting firms and work with them, but don't use them exclusively.

CAREER-RELATED WEBSITES

The sites listed below are job-related websites that will allow you to post your resume online. Keep in mind that this is only a partial list. See Appendix B for a more extensive list of websites.

www.monster.com: **includes over 350,000 job postings plus career, resume, and interview advice.**

www.headhunter.net: **includes over 169,000 job listings plus a career resource center.**

www.jobs.com: **lists job postings from over 1000 companies and includes a student resource and information center.**

www.hotjobs.com: **has a very large database of jobs; visited by over 2 million job seekers per month.**

The Internet

Using the Internet is another good way of getting your resume "out there." However, there are some important things to keep in mind about the Web. First, competition is extremely stiff. For instance, one career website, *headhunter.net,* listed a whopping 169,165 jobs in

February 2000—but the site also reported that almost 360,000 resumes were posted and over 3 million total users accessed the site. Indeed, most of the large career sites boast of millions of users per month.

You should also note that your resume might need to be written and presented in a particular way. If you are submitting electronic resumes to individual firms, you will have some leeway in terms of format and style. Many companies accept electronic submissions of resumes created in word-processing programs like Microsoft Word or WordPerfect. If you use one of these software packages to create a resume, pay careful attention to the format in which the finished document needs to be saved before sending it to an employer. Most employers prefer to receive resumes in ASCII or Rich Text Format, although some may accept .doc files (documents saved in Word format).

Many career-related websites provide a resume template. The majority of online resume templates that you'll come across on various job-related sites (and on sites hosted by individual employers) follow the same basic format as a traditional chronological resume. You'll be prompted to enter each piece of information (from your resume) into specific fields, and you'll most likely be limited to a certain number of fields.

Rather than seeking out specific companies, some people allow the companies to seek them by posting online resumes that can then be scanned by any firm looking to recruit new employees. When employers scan resumes on the web, they are looking for specific keywords.

Keywords are the backbone of any good electronic resume. If you don't incorporate keywords, your resume won't be properly processed by the employer's computer system. Choosing the right keywords to incorporate into your resume is a skill unto itself and takes some creativity and plenty of thought. For example, each job title, job description, skill, degree, license, or other piece of information you list within your resume should be descriptive, self-explanatory, and be among the keywords the potential employer's applicant tracking software is on the lookout for as it evaluates your resume. The keywords you incorporate into your resume should support or be relevant to your job objective. Also keep in mind that employers generally scan online resumes for nouns rather than verbs. While traditional resumes tend to utilize strong action verbs, a scannable resume should include precise, specific nouns. Also, you should avoid using abbreviations and symbols in scannable resumes: type "Doctor" instead of "Dr." and "percent" instead of "%."

If you plan to circulate your resume electronically, but don't know how, get advice from a friend who does or seek assistance from your college career office. You might also want to get a copy of one of the many books on this subject, such as LearningExpress' *Great Resume*. A good resume book will provide step-by-step outlines for writing any type of resume, including online resumes. Finally, the Web itself is a great place to look for tips. Many career websites will provide detailed information about the best ways to utilize their services.

CHOOSING A STRATEGY

The best strategy to get a job interview is to use all strategies. Don't just rely on ads or your college career center—avail yourself of any opportunity or resource that might bring you closer to your goals. After a couple of months of experimenting with different methods of getting interviews, do what any president of a corporation would do: analyze the results. If you've made little or no progress with ads or the database in your college career office, you need to reinvest your energies in more successful strategies. This might involve using a combination of new and old networks, reworking your resume (to give yourself an edge on the Internet), and using the services of more than one recruiting firm. You also might want to try new ideas, such as:

- Going to events sponsored by companies or industries that interest you—such as nonprofit fundraisers or movie previews—with the express purpose of meeting new people to network with.
- Volunteering for a few hours each week in your area of interest; if you are interested in education, for instance, you might volunteer at Literacy Volunteers; those interested in health care might volunteer at a local hospital, while future

accountants might devote their time to the Association for Accounting Administrators.

- Making business cards to hand out while networking (including a private phone number with voice mail and an e-mail address).

Recognizing the X factor

On the other hand, some strategies for getting interviews in *certain fields* are known to be particularly effective. For instance, Internet and technology companies are more likely than other types of firms to use online career sites (such as *monster.com* or *hotjobs.com*) to recruit employees. So, if you're interested in working for an Internet firm, you'll want to check online sites for job listings. However, if you're more interested in working for a small, traditional accounting firm, you might be better off networking or applying for a summer internship with a particular firm.

But no matter what field you are interested in, it helps to know that a number of variables—or unpredictable factors—come into play when you are looking for a job. The business world has its own rules and idiosyncrasies. For example, you might think you have a good shot at a position in a particular company, but someone else, who seems just as qualified as you are, may have an even better chance. Why? The other candidate may have a personal reference from someone who already works at the firm or may have presented his credentials more effectively during an interview. This is another excellent reason to spread your net as far as possible, so you can increase the number interviews you land. The more interviews you have, the more likely you are to get hired.

Networking

One of the most fruitful resources to tap is the people you know: college peers, friends and family, or people from your past, such as high school teachers or community leaders. Even the contacts you made in certain clubs or activities in high school can be helpful. For example, it might be possible that the former editor of the school literary magazine or newspaper is now in a position to help you find a job in publishing. The beauty of asking people you know to be resources is that they are easy to talk to and know something about you and your strengths; they will also be genuinely interested in helping you.

Once you begin networking, you will likely be surprised to find out how many connections you have. Your Aunt Erma's tennis partner may just happen to have a son who knows the editor of the magazine you're dying to work for. Or, your high school principal might be able to tell you that his wife has an opening for a paralegal at her law firm. Although all of your friends may work in the computer industry, you may find that some of *their* friends are artists, editors, accountants, brand managers, or investment bankers.

The biggest obstacle to using networking as a resource is resistance. Many people, even seasoned executives, are shy about networking. To them it seems like asking for help without giving anything back. But networking really isn't about asking someone for a job—it is simply a means of getting information and gaining a little visibility for you at the same time.

One drawback to networking, at least in the beginning, is that it restricts you to the limitations of other people's connections. If they don't know very many people, or if the people they *do* know aren't in a position to help you, your research will be limited.

Despite some of the obstacles associated with networking, it's important not to underestimate the value of talking to the people you know about their careers. Even if your high school principal's wife, the attorney, isn't looking for any new paralegals, she may be able to talk to you about the field of law in general or the job of a paralegal in particular. These discussions can be very helpful in introducing you to industries that you are not familiar with or eliminating certain fields from your list of possible career choices.

So, talk to the people you know. Next, make a networking list based on the people *they* know. Then start making calls. See Chapter 3 for more information about networking.

"I don't think I would have gotten my job if I hadn't put so much time into networking. I was very interested in working in a museum, but those jobs are hard to find and you have a much better chance of landing one if you have some connections. I must have called everyone I knew—and everyone they knew! It took dozens of calls, but I finally found the contact I was looking for: my uncle's golf partner's wife was a curator at a large, metropolitan museum—and it turned out that she was looking for a personal assistant! If I hadn't invested the time into making those calls, I never would have found this job." Nathaniel, Personal Assistant

Putting Together a Target List

Before you pick up the phone, take some time to brainstorm and make a target list. A target list contains all the names of the people you know who might be able to help you get a job in the field you are interested in. Fortunately, making such a list isn't hard to do. Start with your own family. Who are the people your mother, father, or siblings know? You'll be surprised how many good connections they have. If your mother teaches in a high school, don't assume that she doesn't know anyone that could help you. After all, she knows the principal and other teachers—and these people may have spouses or friends who may be working in the field or industry that interests you.

Take your list of network contacts and a pen wherever you go. A name that you suddenly think of while you're stuck in traffic or waiting in line may be valuable.

So, think creatively and don't make the mistake of eliminating names before you've written them down. Put everybody you can think of on your list, and, again, resist the temptation to edit the list before you start making calls. Don't forget to include addresses, phone numbers, and job titles whenever possible. In fact, now would be the ideal time to devise a system for network record keeping. It doesn't matter if you use a computer, Palm Pilot, index cards, or a notebook, as long as you keep your list up to date. This network is an invaluable resource that you will replenish and go back to again and again over the course of your professional life.

Now, go back to the first person on the list—your mother, say— and write down all the names and information she gives you. Encourage her not to edit the names on *her* list! She may be just as surprised as you are by how well connected—and potentially useful—some of her friends and colleagues are.

NETWORKING ADVICE FOR THE SHY

1. **Practice, practice, practice.** Rehearse what you'd like to say before dialing a number or going to a meeting. Write down sample openings or questions and practice saying them.
2. **Listen up.** If listening is your strength, then use it. Pay close attention to what your contact says and use the information you get as fodder for more questions or segues into further discussion.
3. **Take it slow.** Give yourself lots of time to work on finding a job. Begin networking with the people with whom you feel most comfortable—family and close friends. As you get more networking practice, you'll feel more comfortable contacting individuals you don't know as well.

Remember that your target list is not for one-time use. Keep it alive and active by constantly adding names. It's not unusual to have as many as 75 contacts at one time, but don't feel daunted if you have only 6 people in your network. By the time you finish brainstorming with family and friends that number might jump to 30 or more.

An important thing to remember is that getting a job is a full-time job in itself; so don't be surprised if you make ten calls—or even dozens of calls—every day. You can run through your list quickly at this rate, which is why it is important to keep replenishing it with more names and numbers; ask everyone you network with for additional contacts. Of course, you'll be answering ads, going to your college career center, and checking in with your recruiter at the same time.

Now that you have a target list, analyze it carefully. If you know what industry or field you want to work in, prioritize your list: determine where the greatest opportunities for employment are and check off those names first. But before you make contact with anyone, establish what it is that you want—what kind of information are you looking for? Do you want to make contact only for information or, ideally, would you like the connection to result in a job? Of course, as mentioned earlier, networking really is all about information—getting in touch with people who don't necessarily have a job to offer, but who are willing to share their knowledge about the industry or field they work in. You might want to ask:

- What types of jobs are available in a particular field
- What the salary ranges are for those jobs
- What sort of day-to-day duties are involved in a certain job
- What qualifications are necessary to enter a specific field
- Whether you'll need more training to get a job in a particular area
- Based on your credentials, would the company see you as a viable candidate

In all likelihood, these questions will lead to more questions when you actually speak with your contacts. And always be sure to ask whether your contact can put you in touch with another individual who might be willing to discuss his or her job with you.

Networking is also about visibility—getting yourself "out there." If you find out about an actual job opening through your target list, you are ready to start interviewing. (Chapter 5 has more specific information about interviewing.) Whatever you decide, think carefully about what you want to say and the questions you'd like to ask. Then write them down.

....

Mary Burns is interested in a job as a paralegal. She learns that her older brother has a good friend named John Elia, who is an associate at a large law firm. Mary decides to give John a call. Below is a sample dialogue that might be part of their conversation.

Mary: **Hello, Mr. Elia. My name is Mary Burns, Harvey Burns's younger sister. I've just graduated from Gateshead College and I'm very interested in the legal profession. Frank suggested that you might be a good person to talk to about the field.**

John: **Sure. I'd be happy to talk with you. What would you like to know?**

Mary: **First, I was wondering if you could tell me a bit about the qualifications required to become a paralegal.**

John: **That really depends on where you want to work. Many firms, large and small, are interested in hiring people right out of college. Large firms even recruit on campus. They're looking for people with strong academic records, and good communication and organizational skills. There are also a number of paralegal training programs available at colleges around the country.**

Mary: **Do most of the paralegals at your firm have specific paralegal training?**

John: **No. My firm tends to hire people right out of school. I think paralegal programs are more popular in some areas of the country than others, but I'm not the best person to ask about that.**

Mary: **And what are the general job responsibilities of a paralegal?**

John: **In a large corporate firm, your primary responsibility is document management. Corporate cases can involve hundreds or even thousands of boxes of documents, and you have to organize them, keep track of them, distribute them to lawyers, etc. You'd** also be editing briefs, preparing exhibits, and handling clerical duties, like photocopying and data entry. At a smaller firm, you'd probably have greater responsibilities. You'd actually get to write up briefs and other court documents. The downside is, you'd probably be making less money.

Mary: How much do paralegals make?

John: It varies by firm. In a big city, it would be around $25,000–$30,000. The good news is, you'd also be making a lot of overtime pay, which could add anywhere from $5,000 to $15,000 to your salary.

Mary: Is your firm currently recruiting?

John: Sure. We hire year-round. Why don't you fax me your resume, and I can let you know if you have the skills and experience we typically look for in paralegals. I'm not involved in hiring, of course, but I can let you know whether or not you'd be suited to a firm like mine.

What You've Learned

Mary has learned quite a bit during this conversation. This information will not only help her when interviewing with John Elia's firm but with any other corporate firms.

It's important to analyze the information that you receive and record it in a notebook. When you get to Chapter 4, Preparation and Success Stories, you will want to make a link between what you've learned during the informational interview and how you will present your credentials.

Get a pencil and write down all the pertinent information that Mary can use during the next phase of the interview. Now compare your list to the list below:

1. Qualifications for a paralegal in a large and small corporate firm require a strong GPA, good communication skills, and organizational ability.

2. Responsibilities include document management, requiring attention to detail, organizing and prioritizing, using tracking systems, and interacting with different attorneys, as well as editing, preparing exhibits, and routine clerical functions.
3. Some colleges have paralegal training programs.
4. In large cities, salary can be $25,000–$30,000 plus overtime. (It is important to ask the average hours of overtime per week so you can determine your total compensation package.)

Now, the interview has left you with a list of to-dos. Pretend you're Mary, and write down a list of to-dos. Then match them against the list below:

1. Send a thank-you note to John Elia. (You may write or e-mail this note. In any case, it's helpful to get John's e-mail address for future correspondence.)
2. Fax a resume and cover letter to his attention.
3. Tell your brother you spoke with John Elia. (John may speak with your brother and you don't want him to be caught off guard.)
4. If you don't hear from John in one week, call back to follow up.
5. If John sets up an interview with you, read Chapters 4 and 5 right away.
6. See if you have an opportunity to interview on your campus. Go to your college campus and see when the large law firms are recruiting. If you've missed the date, ask for the name of the contact person at the law firm and send your resume.
7. Find out if your GPA is competitive with students who have been hired by other law firms. Your college career center may have the GPAs for alumni who have found jobs in law firms.
8. Determine whether you'd be happier in a large or small law firm. Go to your college alumni office. Ask for a list of alumni who work for corporate law firms. Pick a couple

from a large firm and a couple from a small firm. Talk to those alums about the advantages of each.

9. When speaking with alums, take the opportunity to ask them what they felt was the most useful in landing their current job and if they could introduce you to the recruiting person in their firm, providing you're interested.

10. Find out which colleges have paralegal training programs; investigate whether or not firms will require you to have further training and whether or not your chances of being hired will increase if you have taken some classes in the field.

Getting ready to make the call

When you are ready to make contact there are at least three good ways to go about it:

- Call the person yourself
- Write a letter or e-mail to the person
- Ask the person who referred you to call, write, or send e-mail

If you've never networked before, a safe way to start is to call someone with whom you feel comfortable. Decide how you'd like to open the phone call before you actually dial. Some possibilities include:

- Hello, Ms. Walker. My name is Elliot Bruno. I'm George Bruno's nephew. I'm interested in learning more about the field of equity research, and my uncle suggested that you might be a good person to talk to. If you have the time, I'd very much like to meet for a few minutes sometime next week.
- Hello, Ms. Walker. I'm Elliot Bruno, George Bruno's nephew. I'm interested in pursuing the field of equity research, and

Uncle George mentioned that you work in that field. Do you have a few minutes to discuss your job with me?

- Hello, Ms. Walker. My name is Elliot Bruno. My uncle, George Bruno, worked with you at Harmon & Associates. He suggested that you might be willing to talk with me about your job doing equity research. I'm interested in pursuing a job in this field, but I'd like to learn a bit more about it. Is there a good time to call you and chat for about fifteen minutes?

If you're feeling a little shaky about calling someone you don't know, write a letter or send an e-mail. This will give you more time to develop your thoughts and ask important questions. A typical letter might look like this:

April 10, 2000

Ms. Pamela Walker
Blackstone & Company
117 West Pine Road
Harmony, RI 69131

Dear Ms. Walker:

My uncle, George Bruno, one of your former colleagues at Harmon & Associates, referred me to you. I am a recent college graduate interested in pursuing a career in equity research. I was wondering if you would be willing to talk with me briefly about your experiences in this field. I will call your office to see if we can arrange a time to chat in the next few weeks. You may also feel free to call me at (914) 555-3774. Thank you for your time and assistance.

Sincerely,

Elliot Bruno

If you feel especially insecure about contacting someone on your list, ask the person who referred you to write or call for you. This will break the ice, making it easier for you to follow up with a note or phone call of your own.

Be Proactive

Never wait for a potential contact to call *you*. If you write a letter, remember that you will likely have to make a follow-up call. This will also be true if you've asked someone else to make the initial contact. If you leave a message for a contact and do not hear back, don't be afraid to call again. Your contacts are busy people who have deadlines and obligations to meet. They may forget to call you back, but that doesn't mean that they are unwilling to speak with you. This is *your* job search, and you should expect to do most of the work involved.

....

Learning to build a network is a skill that will serve you for life. Networking's primary objectives are:

1. **To get general information about the industry, company, or field in which you are interested**
2. **To get specific information about a job or career**
3. **To raise your visibility in the job marketplace**
4. **To expand your professional network that you will rely on for ideas, resources, and support throughout your career**

....

Making the call

Okay, you've thought about what you want to ask—you know what you want to know about—and you're feeling confident. Now's the time to pick up the phone and call someone on your target list.

You'll be surprised how well things go, especially if you've thought about what you want to say. Once you've introduced yourself, you can get into the purpose of your call. But first it's important to build a little rapport; you want to start a conversation, not an interrogation. A good way to do this is to ask the person a few questions about his or her life and career, such as:

- How did you choose your field?
- What advice would you give to someone starting out in this field?
- What made you successful?
- What mistakes do people make in your field?

When the person you're talking to tells you about his career path, listen with one ear, but with the other try to pick up on the links between your experience and his. Instead of launching immediately into the next question look for a natural place to interject yourself: If you can say something about your own life that relates to the experience of the person with whom you are conversing, so much the better. For example, if the person you are interviewing—say he's a CFO—tells you that he started his career as a bank teller, it builds rapport to tell him that you are working part-time as a teller yourself. Or if the person you are speaking with just happens to mention that she owned her own business before going into corporate life, it would be apropos to say that it was your job to put the checks in order when your mother started her business a few years ago. This exchange of "stories" is valuable because it helps build a connection.

Another way to connect with your contact is to smile, even though you're speaking on the phone and not face-to-face. Smiling will make you feel less nervous, and your voice will sound warmer and friendlier.

Of course, you don't want to be overly personal—find a balance between self-revelation and conversation. And don't lose sight of your objectives, which are to get information about the company, the industry, and available jobs. You're also raising your visibility in the job market and doing your homework to find the right career for yourself. The challenge is to convince the person you are interviewing with that you have the skills it takes to be successful *while* you are getting information.

This is what makes the conversation strategic. You want to present your credentials, while simultaneously garnering information from the other person. That's what's going to make him or her call a friend or colleague and say, "Hey, I just spoke to this terrific person over the phone who wants to be a financial analyst. Do you have some time to talk with her?" In the meantime, go ahead and ask a few good general questions. For example, if you are interested in investment banking, you might ask:

- Who are the major players in the field?
- What's the difference between them?
- What is your company's niche?

Next, narrow your questions down:

- Do investment banking firms hire recent college graduates?
- How important is a graduate degree?

If the person to whom you are speaking has had the benefit of seeing your resume, ask him or her:

- Do you think my background is a good fit for this industry?
- Do I need any other skills or work experience to make the fit better?
- If you were I, what would you do next?
- Is there anyone else you feel I should talk to—either inside or outside the company?

One final bit of advice: it is crucial to keep your call to around 10 to 15 minutes. If you meet in person, try to keep it to half an hour, unless the person you're meeting with has more time. You want to get all your questions answered, but you don't want to annoy your contact by taking up a tremendous amount of his or her time. Review your questions before you call and make sure you haven't included any that are extraneous or redundant. Once you're on the phone, stay focused. Even if your friend Hal helped you make the contact, don't spend half the conversation talking about what a great guy Hal is. This will waste both the contact's time and yours. Be attuned to what you hear on the other end of the phone. If your contact sounds frazzled or is being constantly interrupted, set up an appointment to speak with her at another time. It is often helpful to start the conversation by saying, "This will take about ten minutes. Do you have that amount of time to spare right now?"

A WORD ON MENTORING

Mentoring, when an older or more experienced person takes a special interest in someone who is younger or just beginning a career, can occur in almost any field. It is *not* appropriate to ask someone to mentor you if you haven't already established a strong connection through a mutual friend, a colleague, and a member of your family, or on your own. The job of mentoring is rarely taken lightly: it involves a sizeable investment of time, as well as commitment to someone else's career. Mentoring sometimes develops between colleagues and has many benefits. For example, if you are just entering the field of fabric design and another colleague takes a special interest in you by sharing his or her training, experience, and creativity, you will have a distinct advantage over others. This is especially true if your mentor just happens to be a leading light in your field. But mentoring doesn't have to be that dramatic to work well. Very often, it boils down to being given the strategic advice we all need to figure out how to do our jobs better, get promoted more quickly, or move to another department, company, or field.

Sometimes we talk with people and we just click. Recent grads can find mentors during the job search process. If you've met someone with whom you'd like to maintain a professional relationship,

**you can ask, "Given my background, would you be willing to make
an introduction on my behalf?" or "Would you mind if I kept you up
to date on my job search?"**

....

Answering questions

Just when you think you have it made, the person you've been
questioning suddenly asks you a question. Will you be prepared to
answer him or her if you are asked, "What are your career goals?"
or "Why did you choose this particular industry?" The best way to
prepare for this eventuality is to think of your answers ahead of time
and practice saying them out loud. Remember that the person with
whom you are networking has also interviewed people, so the questions he or she will ask over the phone will be similar to those you
might hear on an interview. Just watch out for the dreaded question:
Where do you want to be in five years? And be prepared. (Take a
look at Chapter 8 for other tough questions you might be asked.)
Finally, bear in mind that the person who asks you these questions
is probably genuinely interested in helping you and actually needs
to know the answers. He or she is only trying to learn more about
you, in order to give you the best advice.

Sample Questions and Answers

Below are some questions that you might hear from one of your
contacts, along with sample answers. Remember that networking is
not that different from interviewing: you should be prepared to sell
yourself and be able to speak clearly and concisely about your skills
and interests.

Why are you interested in investment banking?

I'm looking for a job that will let me utilize my quantitative and
analytical skills. I took a number of advanced math courses in college, and I've honed my abilities to work with and understand

numbers. I think that investment banking will allow me to develop these skills further, and give me some great hands-on experience in the business world.

Do you have any experience in advertising?

I've spent two summers working as an intern at the advertising firm of Grouper & Trout. During that time, I worked closely with account executives, and I was able to observe and study the process of taking an idea and turning it into a successful ad campaign. I've also taken a number of computer classes, including desktop publishing, Quark, and HTML. I think that my computer skills will be valuable to agencies.

What do you know about this law firm?

I know that the firm is the third largest in the city, and specializes in corporate mergers and acquisitions. This is the largest office, and you're a global firm with offices in London, Madrid, and Hong Kong. I read recently in the *Wall Street Journal* that you handled the merger of DEF Telecommunications and GHIMail.com. I'm fascinated by how the law applies to growing technology markets, such as the Internet and telecommunications, so I was particularly interested in that aspect of your firm.

Protocols and other advertisements for yourself

After you've put down the phone and collapsed with relief on the living room sofa, pull yourself together and write a thank-you note to the person you've just spoken to. Formalizing your thanks on paper is not an empty, leftover practice from the Victorian era; it is a perfectly healthy convention that is alive and well today.

It doesn't matter if you handwrite or type your note, and if you feel more comfortable expressing your thanks via cyberspace, boot up your computer and send an e-mail message. A thank-you note will show your contact that you genuinely appreciated the information she gave you. It will show her that you are polite and professional. And, as a reminder of your interest in that field, your note may very well go a long way toward influencing her to provide you with more information, names, and so on.

If the person you spoke to over the phone gave you the names of other people to contact—and you got in touch with them—write a second note, thanking the person for giving you the contacts and reporting on the outcome of your conversations. This is an elegant way to close the loop—and it speaks volumes for you. Following up on leads shows initiative, but sending a thank-you note each time one of those leads pays off is an indicator of uncommon courtesy.

Going the extra mile can confer all kinds of extra benefits. For example, during the course of a telephone interview, the administrator of a large urban pediatric hospital mentioned that he liked fly-fishing to the young woman who was speaking with him. At the moment she didn't know what to say. She knew nothing about the sport. But two weeks later, while she was on vacation in Colorado, she picked up a magazine and, lo and behold, there was an article about fly-fishing. She photocopied the article and sent it to him with a little note that said: I remembered how much you like fly-fishing and thought you would enjoy this.

Years later, the administrator to whom the young woman sent the magazine article continues to stay in her network. Anybody would respond positively to someone taking note of his interests. The young woman didn't have to follow up with a magazine article—it wasn't a requirement. On the contrary, sending it was an act of grace—a clear sign of her willingness to give something back.

When you become part of the business world you'll continue to need a network for three critical things: **ideas, resources,** and **support.** If, for instance, you're having difficulty implementing a particular strategy for your company, you may need to call on one of your contacts who has had experience implementing a similar strategy in his firm. Or, if you receive a promotion that entails a number of new responsibilities, you might want to speak with someone in your network who can give you some advice on trouble-shooting. No one is successful alone. And remember that once you start working, it will be much easier to find other jobs and opportunities if you've kept up your contacts. In fact, your list of resources is very like a client list, which makes your network of business contacts a valuable asset to any company. Treat it as such. And when you get that first job, be sure to send an announcement letter to all the people in your network. Tell them where you are and thank them for everything they've done.

Now that you've finished reading this chapter, you should know how to use your available resources to secure your first round of interviews. Don't forget to read the help-wanted ads in the newspaper, search online, check out your college career center, and talk to a recruiter. Remember, when you make critical use of *all* the resources at your disposal, you will be able to learn even more about available opportunities, your chances of landing an interview will be even greater than if you used only one resource. Furthermore, don't forget to use your network. You shouldn't be afraid to call everyone and anyone whom you can think of: It will be a pleasant surprise to discover how many people have helpful information or advice concerning your job hunt. Your biggest goal should be to get the word out everywhere that you are searching for a job—the network you begin to build and use now will be one of the richest veins to tap for resources, ideas and support in the future.

AN INTERVIEW SHOULD BE
A CONVERSATION, NOT A MONOLOGUE.

Pearl of Wisdom

"I interviewed one recent college graduate who was intent on selling himself to me—even if that meant not letting me get a word in edgewise. I could hardly get out a question before he would launch into a long monologue about his qualifications. I knew in five minutes that I wouldn't hire him—we need individuals with good listening and interpersonal skills. Of course, I want to hear about candidates' skills and abilities, and I like to hear stories that illustrate their claims, but an interview is a two-way street. You can't just come in ready to talk. You also have to be ready to listen, and you have to prove to your interviewer that you can conduct a conversation with grace and professionalism."

—JOAN, HUMAN RESOURCES DIRECTOR

CHAPTER 2

first impressions

Your Resume and Cover Letter

THE MOST EFFECTIVE tool in your job-acquisition kit is a professional resume that highlights your experience and accomplishments. You'll want to give copies of your resume to contacts in your network, so that they can assess your skills and pass your information along to others. But, even more to the point, you'll need a resume and a well-written cover letter just to get a foot in the door for an interview. Your resume will be an interviewer's—or an employer's—first impression of you, and it will be the deciding factor in whether or not you get an interview.

Creating a resume can be a challenging task: How do you condense your skills and experience into a single, one-page document and still manage to express what is most unique about you? Putting together a winning resume-plus-cover-letter package, like all aspects of the job search, requires a little preparation.

Before focusing on the mechanics of resume and cover letter writing, give some thought to your previous work experiences. Whatever you do, don't assume that certain jobs don't "count" in the marketplace. You'll discover that the secret to writing a good resume lies in the telling of *accomplishments* rather than *tasks*.

WHAT'S SO SPECIAL ABOUT YOU?

The biggest mistake most people make in writing resumes is focusing on job responsibilities, instead of emphasizing *accomplishments* on the job. At the same time, you want to be pragmatic and show prospective employers that you have already demonstrated some proficiency in the very skills they are looking for, no matter what kind of work you've done. This is especially important for students and recent college graduates whose work experiences, at first glance, might seem limited or unmarketable for one reason or another. These obstacles, however, can be overcome.

For example, if you worked as a nanny when you were in college you might be tempted to think that the experience was limited in terms of marketable skills. But you'd be wrong. If the terms you use in your resume are relevant to the job you want, you can translate "taking care of kids" into "business skills." How? It's largely a matter of using the right vocabulary. First of all, don't overemphasize the obvious tasks for which you were responsible as a nanny, such as watching three small children and opening the family house in Martha's Vineyard, etc. No doubt it takes a lot of organization, planning, and responsibility to take care of three children, but what are some of the other skills you developed and put into use? Did you have certain budgetary responsibilities as a nanny? In all likelihood, you did. So, if the job you want is in a financial services industry, for example, you'll want to emphasize your experiences with money management. The chart below shows other ways you might capitalize on your experiences as a nanny.

ACTIVITY	SKILLS LEARNED	JOB SOUGHT
Handling weekly grocery shopping	Budgeting, accounting	Financial industries and services
Taking kids to camp or lessons; planning daily activities	Scheduling, time management	Office administration
Coming up with daily activities: games, art projects, etc.	Creativity, problem-solving, persuasion	Advertising
Managing daily chores, household management	Organization, management, project management	Paralegal, administrator, human resources

Capitalizing on what you've already accomplished

Another way to maximize your work experience on a resume is to be very specific about what you've already accomplished. For example:

- If you want to emphasize your leadership qualities, don't just say that you were the editor of your college newspaper. Itemize your accomplishments. For example, you met tight deadlines—in fact, didn't miss a single one—and published 32 editions of the paper over a nine-month period, etc. This will tell your interviewer that you are already well organized, and know how to meet certain business expectations.
- If you are interviewing for a job in a food-related industry, don't just say that you were a writer for your college newspaper. Instead, emphasize the fact that you covered the food beat for two years and wrote at least one story a month. This will be an especially resonant detail if, for example, your interviewer loves gourmet dining and is an avid reader of *Bon Appétit*.

The more you can say about your experiences, some of which might not seem that valuable to you at first glance, the better—as long as you describe them in a way that enhances your viability for a particular job. Make your accomplishments jump off your resume, rather than assuming that the interviewer will pick them out. The interviewer is not a mind reader. The only information she will have is the information that you provide in your resume, so make every word count.

GETTING STARTED: THE NITTY-GRITTY OF RESUME-WRITING

Your resume should include some basic information:

- Your contact information (your name, address, email address, phone number, fax number, cell phone number, etc.)
- Education history, including any awards or honors or time spent studying abroad
- Employment history, including internships
- Special skills (such as advanced computer skills or proficiency in a foreign language)

If you're a recent college graduate, or still in school, you'll also want to list some of the college activities in which you participated, such as student government, sports teams, clubs, or organizations. Any volunteer work should also be listed in this section.

Remember that your resume should be concise. You want to give potential employers a clear picture of yourself and the skills you could bring to a job, but you don't want to overburden them. No employer is going to sift through pages and pages that catalogue your experiences. Don't feel obligated to include every job you've ever had and every organization you've ever joined. If you were a member of the drama club for only one semester of your freshman year, don't include drama club in your Activities section. Extraneous and irrelevant information will only detract an employer from your skills and strengths. Most headhunters and professionals advise young professionals to keep their resumes to a single page. If your resume is longer than the sample on the next page, see if you can delete any unnecessary details.

THE P-A-R RESUME FORMAT

For students and recent graduates, completing the Employment History section is often the most difficult part of writing a resume. One of the best ways to tackle this important part of the resume is to learn the P-A-R format.

What is it?

The P-A-R format is a resume writing format designed to highlight your work experience by emphasizing three things:

1. Basic job responsibilities of previous positions
2. Accomplishments that resulted from your job responsibilities
3. Value-added, or the ways your past employers benefited from your accomplishments

As stated earlier in the chapter, most resumes focus on job responsibilities. The P-A-R format focuses on job results by *specifically describing* your work experience in terms of:

Problems (solved)-**A**ctions (taken)-**R**esults (accomplishments).

In other words, the P-A-R format enables you to sell your credentials in terms of your ability to problem-solve, to take initiative, and, most importantly, to get results.

Chloe T. Katz

1411 Valley Ranch Road
Apartment 10A
Phoenix, Arizona 85253

Cellular: (813) 555-8312
Home: (602) 555-8908
E-mail: chloe@mailnet.com

Education 1995–1999	**Blackmoor University**, Tempe, AZ Bachelor of Arts in History, May 1999 Cumulative GPA: 3.62. • Earned distinction in the history major. • Elected President of Blackmoor Debate Association; directed three tournaments annually, the largest accepting over 400 students.
Experience *1999–present*	**Waterman & Arnoff, LLP**, Phoenix, AZ *Strategic Change Consultant, Consumer and Industrial Products* Responsible for providing consulting services on business development for consumer and industrial products firms and mass market retailers. Perform primary and secondary research, conduct qualitative assessment and quantitative benchmarking. Interact regularly with clients to validate assumptions and to present findings. • Developed new retail channel strategy for private label department in top-ten grocery company. • Evaluated potential revenue for internal software development project, resulting in the establishment of software's market price and an overall 30% increase in revenues. • Focused annual company objectives for large retail organization by performing cost benefit analysis and comparing results to activities of appropriate competitors.
Summer 1998	**Byrne Investments,** Phoenix, AZ *Latin America Mergers and Acquisitions* General duties included researching private and public companies throughout Latin America as potential acquisition targets for buy-side mandates and potential buyers for sell-side engagements. • Identified potential strategic opportunities for expansion for an international cosmetics firm. Researched strategic investment partners and introduced them to the firm's senior management team. • Developed and expanded new product-line activities in Chile and Brazil for a joint venture of U.S. and Latin American clothing manufacturers, resulting in increased sales.
Summer 1997	**Banque Chevalier**, Geneva, Switzerland *Intern, Portfolio Management*

Responsible for valuations of public and private companies to determine intrinsic net worth. Wrote reports with recommendation for buying, selling, and holding to investment management group. Assisted in creating marketing materials and presentations for prospective and current clients.
* Researched twenty medium and large corporations in the United States, Europe, and Asia to analyze their financial fundamentals and reach a market valuation.

Summer 1996   **Le Clotherie**, Scottsdale, AZ
Sales Associate
Responsibilities included customer service, inventory control, and meeting sales quotas for a high-end department store.
* Assisted customers in selecting and purchasing merchandise throughout the fifth largest store in the United States with daily store sales averaging $80,000 per day

Computer Skills   Microsoft Office, Powerpoint, Lotus Freelance and Notes, Aldus PageMaker, Adobe Illustrator, HTML

Languages   Native Spanish speaker, proficient in French

REFERENCES AVAILABLE UPON REQUEST

Note: Because the page size of this book is smaller than the standard 8½" x 11" resume page, this sample is set as two pages. Your resume should be one page.

If you're sending employers hard copies of your resume instead of submitting resumes electronically, be sure you pay attention to the details.

- Choose a high-quality resume paper in a neutral color like white, off-white, or pale gray. Avoid textured or brightly colored paper. Make sure to buy matching envelopes.
- Choose a font that is simple and legible. Use a ten-point or twelve-point font in the body of your resume.
- Format your resume in a simple, easy-to-read way. Intricate formatting or too many font sizes and styles will be distracting to the reader.

A good way to illustrate the concept behind the P-A-R format resume is to go back to the nanny illustration of a few pages ago. Let's say there was a wide age span in the three children under the nanny's care and that her problem was entertaining all of them, despite their different interests. What action might she have taken to overcome this obstacle? Well, first she took the initiative to find an activity that at least two of the children would enjoy. She arranged for them to attend an art class at the local elementary school, while the third child, an avid basketball player, enjoyed her favorite sport in the school playground. The result was that all three children were well entertained and learned new things at the same time. Not bad! The nanny fulfilled the basic requirements of her job by looking after three children and keeping them entertained. But her accomplishments were various: The children were not only taken care of, they were given opportunities to both learn something new and be creative. For the parents—the nanny's employer—the "value-added" was the knowledge that their children received more than they'd bargained for (a nanny who would "just do the job"). Instead they were the beneficiaries of an employee who showed initiative, excellent management and problem-solving skills, and good judgment. Meanwhile, the college student, who accomplished these things, probably didn't consider them useful work experiences at all.

Or take the case of the discouraged graduate who says his college job was "nothing much"—just clerking in a retail store over the holidays. In fact, this experience is quite marketable. Why? Because if you are a sales associate in a store at a high volume time, there are many skills you have to master quickly, such as teamwork, how to provide customer service, and how to "learn" the merchandise. All of these are problems. How did the young man solve them? First he had to act: on occasion, he may have had to delegate responsibility to others, or he may have taken charge of tense situations when they arose between shoppers and overworked cashiers, or perhaps it was his job to reorganize the stock room for more efficient use. It doesn't really matter what action he took to resolve any of these problems, as long as the outcome, whether it was better customer service or increased sales, was positive. All businesses have problems and expect the outcome of their employees' actions to be successful. If you use terms and phrases such as "problem solving" or "teamwork" to talk about your work experiences, you already sound as if you're in business. And that's a big plus.

The benefits of P-A-R

Screening resumes is an essential part of the hiring process, but it is a formidable challenge for a prospective employer to decide who is best suited for a job when there is limited information for each candidate. Again, most resumes simply state a person's job responsibilities—the day-to-day tasks that he or she was hired to do, such as sorting the mail or handling customer complaints. But two people with the same occupation often get very different results on the job. Yet if that distinction (your skills and accomplishments) isn't made clear in your resume, you might be screened out of the interview pool.

Today's prospective employers are looking for people who do more than their basic job responsibilities—they have to add "value"—just like the nanny and retail-store employee in the last examples. The P-A-R format shows a prospective employer that you can be counted on to do just that: to solve problems when they arise—as they always do—and to take action without being told. In order to showcase these talents, your resume needs to prove that you were, indeed, valuable to previous employers. The P-A-R format helps you prove it by quantifying the results of your actions.

Putting your resume into P-A-R format

In order to quantify your work experience and distinguish it from that of other candidates, your resume should:

- Give employers specific information about what you did and how you did it
- Use numbers to measure your results

For example, suppose your friend Susan worked as a customer service representative in a bank. On her resume, Susan might describe her job in the following way:

Responsible for maintaining a high level of customer service to a base of clients with sophisticated banking needs.

Delivering excellent customer service is a real skill and not everyone can do it. Yet the way the job description is written, it seems as if Susan was fulfilling only the minimum requirements of "maintaining" her accounts. At the same time, by not mentioning sales goals or revenues—the kinds of words you expect to hear from anyone who is in sales—Susan sends her prospective employer the message that, as customer sales rep, she wasn't focused on how much revenue she was bringing into the company. How could Susan meet sales targets if she didn't know her sales goal?

Now let's analyze the entire statement, piece by piece. Put yourself in Susan's shoes and answer the questions that follow:

1. *Responsible for maintaining*
   Questions to ask yourself: Were you maintaining (i.e. just carrying on in the footsteps of your predecessor) or did you do something different to keep in constant contact with your customers? What did you do specifically?

2. *a high level of customer service*
   Questions to ask yourself: How did you know it was a high level? Did your boss tell you? Was there a report? Was it tied to revenue or a percent of increase in sales? Do you have any awards or thank-you letters from customers?

3. *to a base of clients*
   Questions to ask yourself: Who were your clients? How many clients did you have? Were they in similar or a wide variety of industries? Did you increase the client base or did it stay stable? If it was stable, how did you contribute to that stability?

4. *with sophisticated banking needs*
   Questions to ask yourself: What do you mean by sophisticated? Does it have something to do with variety in the portfolio, the size of the account, or the complexity of the services?

Remember, you want to prove that you did the job better overall than the next person because of your actions and the results you achieved. And you can *prove it* because specific actions and quantifiable results speak for themselves.

This is how P-A-R formatting can improve Susan's original statement:

Old way: Responsible for maintaining a high level of customer service to a base of clients with sophisticated banking needs.

P-A-R way: Initiated quarterly Industry Briefings for preferred clients in consumer services area, resulting in the company's highest level of Service Excellence in five years.

How P-A-R prepares you for great interviews

There is another advantage to putting your resume into P-A-R format: It is excellent preparation for job interviews. In fact you can look at your P-A-R resume as an outline, or a summary of your accomplishments. Since most interviewers base their questions on information from your resume, you will be that much better equipped to answer them if you have already organized your thoughts and articulated your accomplishments. This, of course, is what the P-A-R format encourages you to do. So when a difficult interview question comes your way, such as, "So Susan, what do you think was your greatest accomplishment at the XYZ company?" you'll be ready to answer.

....

PROOFREAD, PROOFREAD, PROOFREAD!

Spell-check your resume and triple-check your grammar. Then have a couple of friends or a teacher proofread the resume to catch errors you might have missed. Whether you're submitting a printed resume or an electronic one, spelling errors and careless mistakes could very well cost you an interview.

....

POWERFUL VOCABULARY

When you describe your job experiences, be sure to use strong action verbs to describe your duties and highlight the skills you used on the job. For example, suppose your friend Molly worked as an administrative assistant for a magazine. In the following example, she outlines her duties there, but only lists them. By leaving out the action verbs that stress her own initiative, it becomes merely a job description, rather than what she made out of the position:

Filing, research on competitive markets and customer demographics, product database, clerical duties.

Now look at the difference a few action verbs make:

Reorganized filing system and performed clerical duties to increase office efficiency. Conducted research on competitive markets and customer demographics. Created and maintained product database, increasing productivity in six departments.

Molly's job description emphasizes her initiative and effectiveness on the job. Action verbs help to create a picture of an energetic, dynamic employee.

As you incorporate action verbs into your resume, choose only the ones that work best with your individual skills and accomplishments. Try to refrain from using the same action verb two or more times. Even if you've held the same type of job with several different employers, use different words to describe each of your employment experiences.

....

Tip: **Invest in a good thesaurus. It will be invaluable to you as you plan and write your resume.**

....

One final caveat: If you are creating a scanner-friendly resume, use *nouns* instead of verbs to describe your job experiences. In the resume above, for example, Molly wrote that she "managed files." If Molly were writing an electronic resume, she would instead note that she was responsible for "file management." A search engine looking for power nouns, such as "management," would be satisfied with Molly's resume, giving Molly a better chance of getting her resume on the desk of a human resources professional.

....

You might want to use some of the strong, action verbs below in your resume. Keep in mind that this is not a comprehensive list. Take some time to brainstorm and come up with more words to describe your duties and accomplishments.

Authorized	Edited	Performed
Administered	Established	Planned
Advised	Evaluated	Prepared
Analyzed	Executed	Presented
Authored	Facilitated	Publicized
Balanced	Formulated	Published
Budgeted	Generated	Recommended
Catalogued	Guided	Reduced
Compiled	Identified	Regulated
Completed	Increased	Reported
Composed	Implemented	Researched
Computed	Improved	Restructured
Contributed	Initiated	Scheduled
Coordinated	Integrated	Served as
Created	Investigated	Solved
Delegated	Managed	Streamlined
Designed	Marketed	Strengthened
Developed	Negotiated	Supervised
Directed	Optimized	Trained
Distributed	Organized	Tracked
		Wrote

....

REFERENCES

Choose your references wisely. In general, interviewers want the names of former employers, but if you have only held one or two jobs, you could also include professors, co-workers, professional acquaintances, or even your high school principal. Try to choose people who will be enthusiastic and have knowledge of your skills and abilities. Be sure to ask each individual if he or she is willing to be a reference before giving contact information to employers—your references will appreciate the heads up and can take some time to think about what they would like to say about you. If possible, point your references in a certain direction. For instance, you might say, "The bank seems interested in my leadership ability. Can you talk about the time I took the lead with the group research project you assigned?"

You do not have to include your references on the resume itself. Instead, type up a separate list of at least three references and provide all relevant contact information. Make sure to print this list on quality resume paper; and if you're submitting a hard copy of your resume to an employer, make sure you use the same type of paper for both documents.

COVER LETTERS

One of the most common misconceptions among job seekers is that the resume is the only marketing tool to use, and the cover letter is nothing more than an ancillary formality. In reality, your cover letter plays as important a role as your resume in capturing the attention of a potential employer and selling *you* as a viable candidate for a job.

Virtually all employers value an applicant who has strong written and verbal communication skills. Your cover letter will show an employer whether or not you can communicate clearly and persuasively. After all, a resume is typically a series of bulleted lists, phrases, and short sentences, but a cover letter represents an actual writing sample.

Unless you impress an employer with your cover letter first, she probably won't bother to read your resume. In other words, there's a chance your cover letter will be your only opportunity to convince a potential employer that you're a viable job candidate. Both the wording and the overall appearance of your cover letter should complement your resume.

Your cover letter should duplicate only a few bullets of information that are already in your resume. The bullets you select to repeat should match key job information you've received from the ad or informational interviews. Use your one-page cover letter as a marketing tool designed to:

- Introduce yourself
- State exactly what job you're applying for
- State your contact (if applicable)
- Highlight key information on your resume or convey information about yourself that's not in your resume
- Briefly demonstrate why your experience, skills, and accomplishments are a match for the open position and/or that company
- Convince the reader to investigate your resume
- State that you will follow up

The following are some more guidelines and tips that will help you create a professional looking cover letter:

- Follow the format and style of a formal business letter.
- Use a simple font, such as Times New Roman or New Century Schoolbook, throughout your resume; do not use more than one font.
- Use an easy-to-read font size of between 10- and 12-point type that matches your resume. A font size larger than 12 points will look unprofessional, and a font that's printed smaller than in 10-point type will be difficult to read.
- Make sure your cover letter is visually appealing and utilizes white space on the page.

- Try to use standard 1.25-inch left and right margins and 1–inch top and bottom margins.
- Your cover letter should be grammatically correct and contain no spelling errors. Like the resume, use as many action verbs as possible. Make sure you proofread each letter multiple times and ask someone else to proofread it before sending it out.
- Each of your cover letters should be custom written and targeted specifically to the job you're applying for.
- Always personalize your cover letter, using the recipient's full name and title.
- In the salutation, write, "Dear Mr./Mrs./Ms./Dr. (insert recipient's last name):"
- Keep your cover letters to one page.
- It is appropriate to have one-sentence paragraphs within a cover letter.
- You may use bulleted points to keep your cover letter short, yet still get your points across.
- If you're responding to a help-wanted ad or job-opening announcement, state specifically where you heard about the job opportunity. If you're acting upon a referral, mention the name of the person who referred you and their relationship to the reader.
- Avoid using clichés or overly used phrases. There is no need to re-introduce yourself by name in the body of the letter. Throughout the letter, try to be innovative and original with your wording, but not gimmicky.
- Within the first paragraph, specifically mention what position you're applying for. Match the specific job title wording with the wording provided by the employer within the help-wanted ad or job-opening announcement you're responding to.
- Don't lie or stretch the truth in your cover letter.
- Maintain a positive and upbeat tone throughout the letter.
- Make sure your letter flows and that the voice and tense used within the letter are consistent.
- It's not necessary to list your references in a cover letter. However, always bring your list of references to an interview.

- Keep a copy of every letter you send out. Also, keep detailed notes regarding when each letter was sent, how it was sent, and what enclosure(s) were in the envelope.
- Allow ample time, approximately four business days, for your resume package to arrive and be processed before making a follow-up phone call.
- On your calendar, mark the date by which you need to follow up.

Every cover letter should highlight things about you that are of direct interest to the recipient. Before sending a resume and cover letter to an employer, try to develop an overall message and package to market yourself. (See the samples at the end of this chapter.

Finally, remember that your cover letter and resume will give your potential employer her first glimpse of you, so do your best to demonstrate that you will be a proficient and valuable addition to the company. And don't forget to use the P-A-R format to demonstrate your full capabilities: the **Problems** you solved, the **Actions** you took, and the **Results** you achieved in your past experiences. After you have taken all these steps, and supplied yourself with the documents you need, you'll be prepared for the next step: Researching companies and discovering what you want from a job and an employer.

BE ON TIME OR CALL AHEAD

Pearl of Wisdom

"I was meeting a candidate at a restaurant. After I had been waiting outside the restaurant for twenty minutes, he still had not appeared. When he did show up ten minutes later, he just said that he had run late and was sorry. This communicated to me that either a) he didn't want the job, or b) he didn't have good judgment. Yes, emergencies happen, but if you are going to be late, call the restaurant and try to get a message to the person with whom you are meeting. Don't just assume that they will wait for you."

—MARYAM, CONSULTANT

ANDREW K. CHANG
108 Covered Bridge Lane, Caledonia, VT 05007
802.555.9987 akc99@skivt.com

Mr. Ian Zimmerman
Human Resources Director
Peck & Ellis
4 Goldenrod Way
Brattleboro, VT 84295

June 17, 2000

Dear Mr. Zimmerman:

I am writing to apply for the position of paralegal at Peck & Ellis, recently listed at the Brighton University Career Center. My resume is attached for your consideration.

I am a recent graduate of Brighton University, where I received a B.A. in English. As an English major, I developed the written and verbal communication skills that are so essential in the field of law. In addition, I spent a summer internship honing my writing and research skills at Matthew Bender, a publisher of legal books and periodicals.

Prior to conducting a job search, I spoke with a number of entertainment law firms and chose your firm because of the wide range of your clients and your specific paralegal training program. Lee Grantler at Grantler, Smitt & Robinson is willing to speak with you about my skills, diligence, and dependability.

Thank you for your time and consideration. I look forward to hearing from you.

Sincerely,

Andrew K. Chang

January 15, 1999

Janice E. Caruso
Recruiting Administrator
JTI Computing, Inc.
614 East Third Avenue
Columbus, OH 64119

Dear Ms. Caruso:

I write to apply for the position of sales representative at
JTI Computing, Inc., listed recently in the *Ohio Daily News*.
I am a recent graduate of Fitch College, where I received a
bachelor's degree with honors in business and management.

In addition to my strong academic background, I would bring
to JTI Computing:
- Excellent leadership and interpersonal skills, developed
  while serving as editor of the *Fitch College News*, where I
  managed a staff of 45, and as a member of the Fitch College
  Student Association.
- Hands-on sales experience, gained from a summer internship
  at Marlin-Huntley Enterprises, one of Ohio's leading information technology firms.
- Superb organizational and time-management abilities,
  demonstrated by carrying a full course load while working
  20 hours a week for my college computer lab.
- Enthusiasm and a strong desire to learn new skills.

I have spoken with a number of sales and marketing professionals, and I am certain that this is the right field for
me; I am particularly excited about the opportunity to com-
bine a career in sales with my interest in computers and
technology. I am confident that I have the skills and experience necessary to meet the rigorous demands of a competitive and cutting-edge firm such as JTI Computing.

Please see my enclosed resume. I very much look forward to
hearing from you, and I hope that I will be given the opportunity to join your team.

Thank you for your time and consideration.

Sincerely,

Rachel Birnbaum
41 Dover Avenue, Apt. 3C
Columbus, OH 64105
(971) 555-7832
rachelb@mailserve.com

CHAPTER 3

doing your homework

Researching the Company
and Deciding on a Career

IN CHAPTER 1, you learned how to build a network and use your resources to land an interview. By now, you've probably checked out several promising help-wanted ads, searched online career sites, visited your college career center, and done lots of networking. You've undoubtedly sent out many, many resumes and posted your resume online, as well. Hopefully, you've landed at least one interview by now, and maybe many more. If you're still having trouble getting interviews, you might want to review the material in Chapter 1.

Now it's time to prepare for the interview itself. It's always exciting (and sometimes a little frightening) to get ready for the big day. But look at it this way: you've already shown a great deal of resourcefulness, energy, and determination to get this far. A little more planning, research, and advice is all you need to feel confident, relaxed, and optimistic. Think about everything you're learning about yourself and about different industries, organizations, and individuals. You've already begun your professional life.

HOW RESEARCH CAN WORK FOR YOU

As the saying goes, knowledge is power. You will definitely feel more in control and be better prepared for an interview with *any* company if you take the time to research it. For example, is the company profitable? What are its revenues? What are its services or products? How are they marketed? Is the company in expansion mode or maintenance mode? What jobs are available? What kind of a feeling do you get about the company from their various publications?

Keep in mind that your interviewer will ask you what you know about the company. If you haven't done your homework, the interviewer will be able to tell—and it will be a strike against you. Before you have an interview with *any* company, there are three important areas to research first.

- **Sources of information in general.** If you read the newspaper regularly, you may already know a bit about a company that interests you. To learn more, go to the library to find recent articles about the firm in a variety of newspapers, magazines, and trade publications. Has the company been in the news because of an imminent merger or takeover? If so, pay attention to any information or speculation about changes at the top or layoffs. Knowledge of the company's history, especially current events, will serve you well during the interview. You may want to ask, "What's the likelihood that people will be laid off after the merger?" or, "I know that there will likely be layoffs if the merger goes through. If I join the firm and I am laid off, will I be eligible for severance pay?" If the company you are interested in is testing any new products, find out what they are and whether any of them are controversial. Don't hesitate to ask tough questions—it will show your interviewer that you've done your homework and know about the company. It will also show that you are not afraid to ask difficult questions.

- **Trade sources.** If you already have some general knowledge about a company, but want information about a specific job—direct mail coordinator, say—within a specific division of the company—new product development, for example—you will have to dig a little deeper. Once again, go to the library for trade publications or access the Internet for more detailed information. Read trade sources for industry news, such as who just got promoted. Your knowledge will make you sound like you're already an insider.

- **Inside sources.** People are a resource you just can't beat for information about a company. Find an insider who will tell you what the company's *real* benefits—and detractions—are. It can make all the difference between going with a company and running in the opposite direction.

INTERNET BASICS

One of the easiest, fastest ways to research a company is to use the World Wide Web. The Web offers a wide variety of data and allows you to do research at any time of the day or night. If you don't have Internet access at home, go to your college computer center or to a local library.

If you're already comfortable using the Internet, skip this section; but, if you've had little or no experience online, you'll need to brush up on the basics.

Exactly how do you find out what you need to know on the Internet? How is it possible to sort through the vast amount of information it offers and glean just what you want? These are very good questions that you'll need to have answered before you can be proficient on the 'Net.

To access the Internet from your home computer, you need an Internet Service Provider (ISP). Some ISPs, such as America On-Line (AOL), charge a fee for their services and usually include mail servers, which allow you to send and receive e-mail. Other ISPs, such as Juno and NetZero, are free of charge. Check your local phone book or newspaper for local ISPs, or use a library or school computer to get information about other ISPs.

You'll need a modem to connect to your ISP. A modem is a device that allows you to transfer information to and from your computer via your phone line. Remember when you're buying a modem that quicker is better. The faster your modem, the faster you will be able to receive and send information. You'll pay a little more for a faster modem, but you'll save yourself a lot of time and frustration. In many areas, cable companies offer cable modem service, which is a fast digital connection over your cable line. Some phone companies also offer DSL service, which allows simultaneous voice and digital communication over one phone line. If you decide to use a school or library computer, you don't need to worry about ISPs or modems. Just find a computer with a Web browser, such as Netscape, and you're ready to search.

Some large Internet service providers include Web channels that sort the information on the Web into groups, such as computing, news, finance, etc. When you click on any of the channels, you'll find a submenu of what's available.

If you prefer, you can use a Web search engine to find the information you need. Just type in the name of the company you wish to research, or other keywords, and click "Search." Some of the major search sites, and their web addresses, are listed below.

- **Yahoo:** recommended for researching broad general topics. It can be accessed at *www.yahoo.com*
- **Alta Vista:** recommended for precise and complete searches. It can be accessed at *www.altavista.com*
- **Lycos:** recommended for advanced searches; very thorough. It can be accessed at *www.lycos.com*
- **Excite:** recommended for searches on broad, general topics.

It can be accessed at *www.excite.com*

- **Infoseek:** not as large as some other sites, but very accurate. It can be accessed at *www.infoseek.com*

- **Dogpile:** when you enter a search, this website provides results from all of the search engines listed above, as well as many others; extremely comprehensive, although it takes some time to sift through the results of your search. It can be accessed at *www.dogpile.com*

Finding the Information You Need Online

Once you've landed an interview with a particular company, the first thing you'll want to do is check out its website. The site will give you a general overview of the company—i.e. what its general business is and what its products and services are. The website should also give you detailed information about the company's employees, history, and policies. In addition, it may include statistics, newspaper articles, and press releases. Even the design of a website can give you important information (if on a more subliminal level), about a particular company—for example, does it look conservative or cutting edge?

If you can't find a website for a particular company, give them a call and ask whether or not they have a site. A company's site may have an unusual name, making it difficult to find. Or, the firm may not have a website. Although more and more companies are putting information online, some companies may not have their own sites. If this is the case, don't worry.

There are plenty of other ways to find information about a company, if you can't find it on its website. You can search for relevant articles on newspaper sites. For instance, the *New York Times* website (*www.nytimes.com*) allows you to search its archives for newspaper articles, although it will cost you $2.50 to purchase a complete article. The *Washington Post* website (*www.washingtonpost.com*) charges $2.95 per article, but provides free access to articles published in the last two weeks.

Be sure to check these and other major newspaper sites. Your interviewer will be impressed if you can say, "I read in the *New York Times* last week that your company has decided to . . . " But don't forget to do your homework. You don't want to get into a discussion about the company if you can't keep up your end of the conversation.

Another good source of information is online news sites, such as *www.cnn.com*, *www.msnbc.com*, or *www.thestreet.com*, a financial news website. These sites give you the freedom to search their archives, some of which are quite comprehensive, for articles on business and commerce. The best part about these sites is that the information is available free of charge.

OTHER RESEARCH OPTIONS

The Internet and the library are superb resources for gathering information about jobs and companies, but there are a few other good options for research, too. For example:

- Look at how the company advertises its products and services. Does it advertise them on television or in magazines? What do the **ads** say about its products and services? To whom are the ads directed? Is there a guarantee or benefit to the consumer?
- Take a look at the company's **annual report** (assuming that it trades on the stock exchange). It should give you lots of information about the company's profitability and career path. It might even give you salary information about senior management and how bonuses are structured. This kind of information tells you which businesses are important—and who and what they invest in.
- Contact the **Better Business Bureau** if you want to know if the company you are interested in has had any resolved or unresolved problems with either consumers or other companies.

- Call the **Chamber of Commerce** for information about the company's role in the community.
- Remember that your **campus career center** may have printed information about firms that interest you, particularly if those companies participate in on-campus recruiting.
- Go back to your **network.** Ask your contacts if they know anything about the companies that will be interviewing you. For instance, if you have a job interview at a particular investment bank, *any* investment banker in your network should be able to give you *some* information about the firm, even if she doesn't work there.
- Finally, don't be afraid to call a prospective employer's **human resources** department or **public relations office—** usually they are more than willing to send you information about the company.

....

REAL-LIFE CASE STUDY:
RESEARCHING A MAJOR CONSULTING FIRM

Michael, a recent college graduate, landed an interview at a major consulting firm for the position of business analyst. Here's how he went about his research.

1. The firm participated in on-campus recruiting, so Michael's first stop was his college career center. Here, he was able to pick up some pamphlets and fact sheets about the firm. This gave him a general idea about the type of work the firm did.
2. Next, Michael got online. On the firm's website, he was able to read about the firm's philosophy, the types of individuals they hired, and the skills required for the job. The website also provided "case studies," detailing how the firm had helped specific clients. Then, Michael read a few articles that were generated by the firm's consultants, as well as some about the firm.

3. Not satisfied with the information he'd found, Michael headed to his school library, where he printed out articles written about the firm in the past six months. He knew that the articles posted on the website would be very positive, and he wanted to see what kinds of articles the firm had chosen *not* to post on their site.

4. Finally, Michael used his network to find the names of two recent graduates from his college who currently worked at the firm. He contacted both individuals and asked them about the work they were doing, their responsibilities, the training they had received, and the firm's culture.

Michael found that his skills, background, and interests were well matched to this consulting firm. When he went to his interview, he was well prepared to discuss the company with his interviewer. Because he had read so many newspaper articles, he could speak intelligently about recent happenings at the firm and ask his interviewer smart questions. Ultimately, he landed the job.

REDISCOVERING YOUR NETWORK

The people who actually work for a company are always the best source of information, so make an effort to talk to as many of them as possible, especially current employees. Listen carefully to what they say about the culture of the organization they work in. Is it a command and control culture, where the bosses have most of the say and subordinates take their directions? Or is the corporate culture more collaborative, with people working in teams?

To identify an employee who can give you information about a company, go back to your network and re-prioritize the names on your target list. Who might have the information you're looking for? This may be a little tricky if you are a recent college graduate and have a relatively limited number of people in your career network. However, it *is* possible to find someone, if you utilize all your resources. If you can't think of a good contact, ask a friend or career counselor to help you brainstorm.

Sometimes serendipity comes into play. For example, suppose you're interested in working at XYZ Pharmaceuticals, but can't seem to find anyone who works there. Frustrated, you take your pile of research materials to the local coffee shop for a relaxed morning of reading and thinking about what you're going to do next. It's a busy Saturday morning at the coffee shop, and you end up sharing a table with a complete stranger. After a couple of minutes you strike up a conversation and discover to your amazement that he works for a pharmaceutical firm. He's able to tell you about the field, and you tell him about your career goals. He's impressed by your enthusiasm and skills, and offers to introduce you to the company's human resources director. Believe it or not, these things do happen.

Even though there are lots of other excellent options for getting interviews, don't forget your network. Keep going back to it and ask if anyone knows someone who works in the company or even the field that interests you. You never know—you just might hear, "I think my sister-in-law's cousin works there." For all you know that person may work for a company you'd never considered, but if there's an opening or you go for an informational interview, you may discover that you really like the company. In the best-case scenario, your interviewer thinks you'd be a great asset to the company and tells you she'll contact you as soon as there's an opening. A couple months later you get a call. This is a compelling reason to stay in touch with the people in your network. Keep your contacts alive, because you never know when they'll pay off.

Brainstorming

If there isn't anyone in your current network that has contacts in the field you're interested in, you need to find fresh contacts. But first, do a little brainstorming with a friend, career counselor, or someone you know from college. If you need to find a contact at XYZ Pharmaceuticals (to use a previous example) what would you do? How would you start to find that person? One answer is to start with *the people you know*. What about:

- *Your college biology and chemistry professors.* It is not at all unlikely that one of them knows someone in the pharmaceutical industry. Think of the strong relationships some university and college science departments have with industrial researchers, commercial laboratories, and pharmaceutical companies in general.
- *Your family doctor.* Physicians usually have a lot of contact with drug manufacturers. Maybe one of them could introduce you to a company rep the next time he or she is in the office. That person may know if a particular company is looking to hire, or if they are aggressively pursuing recent college graduates in general.
- *The pharmacist at your local drug store* has good contacts with various companies and can keep her ears open for any news that might apply to your search for a job.

Taking the challenge

If you are going to be serious and disciplined about getting a job, it's simply not enough to look at your targeted networking list and say, "Oh, gee, nobody here is in pharmaceuticals." This is where a lot of people give up and make the assumption that it will take too much time or require too much effort to find new contacts, leads, and information to get where they want to go. But if you choose to challenge yourself and figure out the best way to get the information you need, you'll be a step ahead of the crowd. Call the human resources department or public relations office at the organization or company you're interested in and ask them if they ever interview at your college or university. Or, go to the campus placement office for the same information. Even if you've already graduated, your college will likely give you access to their resources. Brainstorm. Take your network as far as it will go and use every resource you can think of, from your grandmother's dentist to every search engine on the Web. If you maximize your opportunities to gain information it will only be a matter of time before you succeed at getting an interview for the job you want.

....

Managing your time and setting priorities usually boils down to common sense. If you're scheduled for an informational interview at a company tomorrow, it doesn't make sense to spend all your time writing thank you notes the day before. Instead, use the time to research the company on the Web or read articles about it at the public library.

....

WHAT DO YOU REALLY WANT?

Now that you've become a nimble researcher and know exactly what to ask other people about specific jobs and companies, do you really know what *you* want? In all the excitement of meeting everyone else's expectations have you lost sight of your own? If so, now might be the time to find a quiet place to think about what you expect from a prospective employer. Some of these questions might help you narrow down what you are looking for:

- Does it matter if the company is domestic or international?
- Do you want to relocate or stay where you are?
- Do you imagine yourself working in a small, medium, or large size company?
- What sort of training program do you want?
- What would make the work important to you?
- How much money do you want to make?
- What other benefits do you want?

- What kind of working hours are you looking for?
- Are promotions and other forms of advancement important to you?
- Do you want a lot of individual responsibility, or are you more comfortable working in teams?
- Do you prefer a hands-on boss or someone who gives you a lot of autonomy?
- Do you want to work at a firm that gives you regular reviews of your progress?
- Do you want to interact with clients or vendors?
- Do you want to work in a corporate or casual setting?
- Does it matter to you if the company invests in companies or causes that you find politically incorrect?

Make sure you've thought about and made a list of things you want from an employer *before* you show up for the interview. The reason for this is that you might be tempted to accept the first offer you get, especially if the terms seem unusually generous. Or you might convince yourself that you should take a job, even though it's not exactly what you want, because it's work "you've been doing for a while." Or "the money's too good to turn down." It's human nature to feel conflicted about making hard choices, but it helps a great deal to think about what you want before you have to decide. Don't be caught off guard and accept something you don't want. Think seriously about the things you *do* want from a job and keep them in mind during an interview.

· ·

To help you decide whether or not a company is right for you, make a chart. Put your offers (i.e. company names) at the top of the chart and list the ten things you want from a company, or an employer, in the left margin of the chart. This way, every time you get a job offer, you can check it against *your* requirements. You'll be asked to refer to this chart many times over the course of your job search, so do take it seriously and fill it out as soon as possible.

· ·

TEN REQUIREMENTS FOR THE IDEAL JOB

What You Want	C & P, Inc.	Little, Learner, & Co.	Perkins, Inc.	J & J, Inc.	Boxer Brothers	Fortune 2000	Snow & Snow Realty	Winnow, Bartlett, & Snooks	Walsh Agency	Central Hospital
$35,000+	✓	✓	✓			✓	✓			✓
Profit Sharing	✓	✓	✓			✓	✓		✓	✓
Good Health Plan	✓	✓	✓			✓	✓		✓	✓
Training Program		✓		✓	✓	✓		✓		✓
Relaxed Boss		✓	✓	✓		✓			✓	✓
Promote From Within	✓		✓		✓	✓	✓		✓	✓
Flexible Hours							✓			✓
Small Company	✓					✓	✓		✓	
Close to Home							✓		✓	✓
Casual							✓		✓	✓

MAKING A MATCH

It's one thing to know what you want from a job, but it's another to match your expectations with an employer's. Do your education, training, and work experience match the requirements for a particular job? The only way to know is to do your research, network, and go on employment interviews.

One of the biggest complaints of college recruiters is that graduates have unrealistic expectations about the type of job responsibilities they will have and the salary they will be paid. Some firms factor in your academic record. This is especially true of legal, accounting, and consulting firms. Nearly every organization values practical work experience. One of the ways to "be in the know" is to do your homework.

Isn't it surprising?

Most people have lots of other traits and talents they might not necessarily group with business skills. But it's important to think about them anyway, because they can say a lot about you. There's an interesting story to illustrate this: One day an executive left her office and went into the lobby to greet a candidate. As they left the lobby, the candidate said good-bye to the receptionist, addressing her by name. The interviewer asked the candidate how he knew the receptionist; as it turned out, they had only just met. The candidate had once worked as a reporter, and people found him very easy to talk to. The executive was very impressed with the man's communication skills and knew that he could use those skills on the job. Many of us have skills that are just as remarkable. The trick is to think of the skills we take for granted as marketable assets.

Ask a friend, a teacher, or someone in your family to tell you at least two things that are special about you. What are some of your personal qualities and how do they affect the people around you? Your special qualities don't need to be earth shattering. For example, is there something in your personality that always seems to come out, whether you're doing something as important as addressing a large group or as ordinary as food shopping? Is it your sense of humor? Are you the kind of person who just seems to have good common sense? Do you have stamina—the gift of sticking with something until you get it right? All of these traits have excellent applications in the working world.

What makes you interesting?

An interviewer might be interested in some of the unique or unusual experiences you've had, especially if they tie into a particular skill. For example:

- **Have you ever lived or traveled abroad?** If so, are you familiar with or fluent in another language? Has the experience of spending time in a foreign culture taught you any other skills that might tie into the marketplace, such as the ability to be flexible, respect diversity, and adapt to new and challenging circumstances?
- **Do you have any hobbies, passions, or avocations** that might demonstrate dedication, initiative, or originality? What about your commitment to the neighborhood soccer team or the volunteer work you do for a "Big Brother" or "Big Sister" program? Maybe you have a passion for collecting rare books or you're a Civil War buff. Remember that employers don't necessarily hire human-shaped bundles of skills that are perfectly tailored to specific job requirements. More often than not they are looking for people whose interests outside of work have taught them something that might enrich the company as a whole.

....

"Through my sorority, I did a lot of volunteer work at a children's hospital and local nursing homes. I think this showed prospective

employers that I was a patient person with good interpersonal skills and that I was accustomed to interacting with different types of people. It also showed that, though I was focused on my career, I was attuned to the needs of others. These are important skills to have in the business world."

—LISA, WEB PRODUCER

Be objective about your accomplishments

Most of us are not the best evaluators of our own best accomplishments. You may not think that something you've done is particularly impressive, whereas someone else might think it phenomenal! For example, a young man was embarrassed to tell his interviewer that it had taken him eight years to get through college because of severe financial difficulties. Instead of being shocked or disappointed, the interviewer was favorably impressed! To his mind, the young man's successful struggle to get through college despite considerable adversity was a powerful demonstration of his determination and persistence—two qualities that are highly valued by most businesses.

Fine-tuning your work needs

After you've given some thought to your strongest work assets and the various qualities that make you interesting as a person and valuable as an employee, tighten the focus on your work habits and preferences:

- Do you like to work alone or in a group?
- Do you prefer close supervision or do you prefer to work independently?
- Are you willing to begin as a trainee with limited responsibilities or would you prefer a position where you have your own responsibilities from the beginning?

- How far are you willing to commute?
- Do you prefer to work in a large office or a smaller one?
- Is diversity in the workplace important to you?
- Do you prefer conservative firms or untraditional work environments?
- Do you prefer to keep a regular schedule or would you like flexible hours?
- Would you change location for a job?
- Under what circumstances would you be willing to relocate or commute for a job?

Think as clearly and honestly as you can about what type of job will give you the best experiences; match your requirements with what a particular company offers. Don't accept any job unless your most important professional needs are being met. In other words if you feel very strongly about not moving to another state in order to get a job, don't be seduced by a slightly higher salary, a better title, or a company car. You will be miserable, despite these perks, if you miss your house, family, and friends, and hate the weather. If you hate driving, don't agree to take a job that requires three hours of commuting every day. There's more than a little truth to the old cliché that happy people make happy workers. Make sure that your needs match the company's need for you before you sign the dotted line—you begin by knowing your own priorities.

CHOOSING THE RIGHT JOB

Remember that there's a difference between a job and a career. Deciding how well matched you are with a company may have a lot to do with whether or not it can take you where you want to be in 2, 5, or 10 years. Suppose you have an offer to do graphic design work for a small ad agency. You know you have the skills for the job, but you also know that you don't envision yourself working in graphic design five years from now. In fact, you're much more interested in pursuing a career in market research. If this is the case, you'll want to think hard about whether or not you should take that graphic design job. Will your experience in graphic design help you get a job in market research a few years from now? Will you be giving up other opportunities in your preferred field if you take this job? Training for any job will take up a lot of your time and your employer's. You will be better served by devoting your time and energy to learning about the career you ultimately want to pursue. Be sure to investigate all aspects of a company, including opportunities for advancement and learning new, marketable skills before making a decision. If working at a particular company might hamper your long-term career goals, it's probably not the best place for you.

In this chapter you have learned about many different ways to research a company. Ultimately, your best option is to use *every* available resource to get the information you want, just as in Chapter 1, when you were learning to marshal *all* of your resources to begin the process of job hunting.

The most important part of your job search is finding the right job for you. "The right job" means different things to different people. But a combination of meaningful contribution, challenge, growth, and recognition will be rewarding to most employees. All of these things will lead to more satisfaction and fulfillment in your work.

Pearl of Wisdom

MAKE SURE THAT YOU ARE RESEARCHING THE CORRECT COMPANY.

"I interviewed a young man for an account coordinator position at an e-commerce company. When I asked him if he knew anything about our company, what we do, what we sell, etc., he launched into a fifteen-minute explanation of another company with a similar name (with whom we often get confused). He had obviously done his homework, but unfortunately he was discussing another company. I explained to him that our company's name is called PhatPencil.com not FatPencil.com. He handled the situation with poise, however, by simply laughing it off with a witty comment and requesting further information on our company. I ended up hiring him anyway because he was highly qualified, thought quickly on his feet (and recovered nicely from a sticky situation), and obviously conducted thorough research. I did, however, suggest to him that, in the future, when he sets up other interviews, he should ask whomever he speaks with to spell out the website and company name."

—Raina, Account Manager

before your foot reaches their door

Preparing Yourself for the Interview

NOW THAT YOU'VE rallied your resources, investigated the company, structured a compelling resume and cover letter, and put a great deal of thought into your skills, strengths, personal qualities, work experiences, and job preferences, you are ready for the interview. The difference between an average interview and a great interview is preparation. There will always be unpredictable questions. The purpose of preparation is for you to decide what experiences are the most compelling in demonstrating your talents. It gives you a chance to sort out and choose the best stories to tell and figure out how to tell them clearly and concisely.

The most important thing for you to bear in mind is that the interviewer's main objective is to determine whether or not you are the best candidate for the job. Your main objective is to communicate your skills and accomplishments while determining if this is the right job and the right company for you. Your resume will provide your interviewer with some answers to questions about your educational background and work history, but of all the criteria he'll use to judge your qualifications for the job, none will be more important than your *accomplishments*.

Many companies today, particularly large companies, strive to make the recruiting process more scientific than it has been in the past. These companies have done research to see what factors (such as skills and traits) have made their employees successful. These factors are called "behavioral measures of success" or "success factors."

Every firm values different success factors; the only way to know the specific factors a particular company esteems is to speak with someone who works for this company. However, in this chapter we identify some generic success factors from different companies that are key in a fast-paced, competitive business environment. The best interviewing strategy is to talk about the academic and work experiences that pertain to these generic success factors. As you tell the stories, the company success factors will stand out, showing the interviewer that you are a viable candidate for the job.

CONVERTING SUCCESS FACTORS TO SUCCESS STORIES

The most effective way to talk about your accomplishments is to recast them in the form of stories: Each one must have the power to successfully document and illuminate your successes.

Depending on the job, your interviewer will be looking for certain kinds of success stories that are based on a number of factors, such as your ability to solve problems, think independently, take initiative, or communicate skillfully. The ten "success factors" that most employers expect from job candidates are listed below. Your job will be to weave these factors into your own "success stories."

....

SUCCESS FACTORS

1. **Accomplishments/Getting Results**
2. **Taking Initiative**
3. **Communication Skills**
4. **Problem Solving**
5. **Teamwork and Team Leadership**
6. **Project Management**
7. **Decision Making**
8. **Strategic Thinking**
9. **Innovative Thinking**
10. **Handling Pressure**

....

Make Your Own Opportunities

Learning how to use success stories effectively cannot be over-emphasized. There is simply no better way to showcase your achievements and prove your suitability for a job. It takes some skill to weave success stories into an interview, but this can be done with relative ease if you rehearse them many times *before* you go to the interview and use all of your communication skills to *tell* your stories once you get there. You will have to take some initiative to find openings for your success stories. Even if your interviewer asks you a question that can be answered with a simple yes or no, resist the urge to give a one or two word answer, as in the following example:

Interviewer: Do you think you work well on a team?
John: Yes.
Interviewer: Can you think of any times when you had difficulty working on a team?
John: No.

Instead, take the opportunity to present yourself in the best possible light. Use one of your strongest success stories. The following sample shows how it can be done:

Interviewer: Do you think you work well on a team?

Jim: Yes. I was co-captain of the basketball team in college—it was a great experience, and a great chance to work with my peers outside of the classroom. I would keep track of new strategies, organize extra practices, and arrange social events for the team. I always thought it was important for the team to spend time together off the court—we got to know each other better, and this helped us work together in games.

Interviewer: Can you think of any times when you had difficulty working on a team?

Jim: One incident comes to mind. A member of our team was a bit of a ball hog. If he got the ball in the game, he refused to pass it, and the other team members were getting upset. But I didn't want to single him out or scold him. Instead, I came up with practice drills that involved a lot of passing. I complimented him on his passing ability and told him it was just the sort of thing he could use in a game. And I spoke to the whole team about passing more in games. Well, he got the picture—and because I was supportive instead of confrontational, I didn't end up with a big argument on my hands.

Who would you hire, John or Jim? Jim took advantage of his interviewer's questions by telling stories that showed off his positive traits. Although John might have been a stronger candidate than Jim in some ways, his interviewer had no way of knowing, because John didn't capitalize on the opportunity to illustrate his better qualities.

Making the connection between Success Factors and Success Stories

No matter what kind of work you've done in the past, you can find a success story to match all ten factors. Keep your mind open—

don't dismiss any work experience as insignificant until you've thoroughly examined it. Think about your academic and work experiences in terms of the problems presented, the actions you took to solve them, and the results.

Accomplishments/Getting Results

One of the most common interview questions is: "What is your greatest accomplishment—the thing you are most proud of?" By asking this question, the interviewer is trying to determine if you get satisfaction from achieving results. She may also want to see if you are proud of your accomplishments; being proud of past results will translate into taking pride in your work with your prospective employer.

There are many types of accomplishments you could use to answer this question. For example, completing your education is an accomplishment. Focus on the individual challenge for you or why you're proud of receiving your degree. Perhaps there's a story that illustrates your overcoming an obstacle, such as saving money under difficult circumstances, figuring out how to pass a challenging class, or getting your writing published. What were the results of your efforts? Here is a sample story that illustrates how you could answer the question:

I was extremely happy when I got into my first-choice college, Elmherst—but the scholarship they offered didn't quite cover my needs. Although I had been admitted to several schools, I felt that, for me, Elmherst would provide the best possible education. So, instead of going straight to school, I deferred for a year and spent the time working at a local hardware store. After a few months, I took on a second job waiting tables. It was a very tough year—but I was proud that I stuck to it. By the time September rolled around, I had saved enough money to attend the school of my choice, and I had some solid work experience.

This story tells volumes about the speaker's abilities to persevere, solve problems, and take charge of his career. It also demonstrates that the speaker is goal-oriented, an extremely important trait in the business world, where every action has a purpose and leads to a greater goal.

Good success stories, like the one above, are rich composites of your experiences and skills, so you will have some flexibility in using them; one story should be able to answer a number of different interview questions. For example, if the speaker above was asked not about his accomplishments, but about a time when he took charge or used initiative, his story about saving money for school would apply.

Initiative

In a fast-paced, competitive business environment, it is important to hire people who can take charge—even if the responsibility is not in their job description. Time is an important element in taking initiative: It's about *doing something when it needs to be done*, instead of waiting for someone else to do it first. Consider the following story:

> *I worked on my college literary magazine. Producing the magazine was always an uphill battle. We received most of our revenues from ads, but the number of advertisers was constantly dwindling—and no one seemed to be doing anything about it. I organized a small committee, and we went door to door, speaking with local businesses about our magazine. Sometimes it took a lot of persuading, but once they saw the quality of the magazine and heard about our diverse audience, most businesses were eager to advertise. We raised so much money that we were even able to print the magazine in color for the first time.*

This story brings out a number of the interviewee's good qualities, including team leadership, determination, and, above all, initiative. All of these qualities are highly valued in the business world. An employer wants to hire people who can recognize problems and take independent action to remedy them.

Communication Skills

Your interviewer will be aware of how long it takes you to answer questions: There is a delicate balance between saying enough to get your success stories across and saying too much. Ask your acquaintances what kind of speaker you are: do you tend to go on and on or are your answers short and blunt? Better yet, have a friend or family member conduct a practice interview with you. Tell your "interviewer" to evaluate your speaking skills, and then try to improve your style.

Tell your story clearly to make sure that the interviewer gets your point. Be concise. Don't get sidetracked by focusing on endless details or irrelevant aspects of the story. If you're telling a story about working on your uncle's farm, for instance, don't bother telling the interviewer the names of all the horses you cared for. It's very important to avoid using slang words such as "like" and "y'know" and "filler" words, such as "um," "eh," and "uh." The *only* way to present your credentials well is to prepare prior to the interview—know what you want to say and how you want to say it. Have someone else listen to you and give you feedback. This will help you feel more confident and do your best.

A common interview mistake is beginning every answer with "Ummm . . . " Usually, a candidate uses this opening to stall for time or give herself a few seconds to collect her thoughts. However, there are better ways to give yourself time to think. Don't be afraid to sit in silence for a moment while you prepare your answer. Your interviewer will not be surprised if you need to collect your thoughts. If this makes you uncomfortable, try paraphrasing the question as you begin your answer. For instance, if your interviewer asks, "How would a coworker describe you?" you should reply, "I think that a coworker would describe me as . . . " By repeating the question, you've given yourself time to compose your answer.

Quick! Which sentence sounds more professional?

1. Uh . . . I think that I'd be an asset to your firm because I'm diligent, and, um, efficient and people tell me that I'm, y'know, a good communicator.
2. I think I'd be an asset to your firm because I'm diligent, efficient, and have excellent communication skills.

Problem Solving: Thinking and Working Independently

It's just as important to be able to take directions as it is to work independently. However, when you *do* work independently it's not always smooth sailing. So, when you're thinking of a story to demonstrate independent thinking, focus on the obstacles you had to overcome in order to solve a particular problem. What steps did you take? Here is an anecdote that shows the candidate's abilities to think independently *and* solve problems. In addition, it demonstrates that she is analytical, reflective, and learns from her mistakes.

I worked at the registrar's office during college. My primary responsibility was filing, but the filing system was hopelessly confusing. I came up with a great way to reorganize the files and spoke to my supervisor about implementing my plan. I was thrilled when she approved the plan, and I spent the next week overhauling the old system. That's when my supervisor started getting complaints from another employee, who had a project due. She needed some information from the files, but couldn't find it because of the new filing system. I quickly called her to apologize and gave her a tour of the new system. Then, I wrote a memo documenting how the system worked and gave it to the other employees. They all agreed that it was a better process. I learned that it's not enough just to have a great idea. You have to consider all the ramifications of implementing that idea and keep fellow employees in the loop at the same time.

Innovation

We live in an ever changing world where the past solutions to business problems aren't always effective. Consequently, more and more companies are looking for employees who can "think outside the box." Perhaps you have never thought of yourself as creative because you don't have a special talent such as writing or painting. Yet everyone can be creative in the area of problem solving. Let's say the interviewer asks you, "Tell me a time when you developed a new idea to solve a problem?" This question is different from the previous problem-solving question because it's asking about "new ideas" or how you've applied your creativity when solving problems. Here's a success story that displays the teller's innovative thinking:

> *I was a member of the drama club in college. We put on several plays each semester, but, over time, our audience began to decrease in size. We needed to come up with new ways to draw people to our shows. One day, I was having a cup of coffee in my favorite coffee shop, thinking about the problem, when I hit upon a great idea. What if we could get the coffee shop to provide free coffee and dessert during intermission or offer discounts to anyone present-ing ticket stubs from our shows? In exchange, we could promote the shop in our playbills and on posters. I spoke with the owner of the shop and he was thrilled—he had also been trying to come up with new promotional ideas. Some of the club members were skep-tical of my idea, but the refreshments and discounts worked like a charm—ticket sales improved thirty percent!*

Leadership and Team Playing

So much work today is done in teams that employers often want to know if you can get along with others and get the work done. What have you done in the past that illustrates your ability to work successfully with others?

Remember Jim, the basketball team captain you met earlier in this chapter? His anecdotes about playing on and managing a sports team showed that he was comfortable as both a team leader and a team player. Stories about playing sports, working in small groups in classes, or participating in college clubs and organizations all demonstrate that you work well with others.

Project Management

Just getting through college is a good example of being able to plan, organize, and set priorities, particularly if you were a student who successfully juggled schoolwork, part-time jobs, club activities, a healthy social life, and maybe even volunteer work. Try to think of some specific examples that illustrate your abilities to manage many tasks at once. The following is a story from a recent college graduate:

> I was an editor of my college newspaper, which came out every Friday. On Thursday nights, all of the editors would gather in the newspaper office to make last minute changes, finalize the layout, and so on. Usually, we were there until seven or eight in the morning. There was a lot of fallout from these all-nighters: Some people weren't prepared for their Friday classes. They fell behind in their reading and turned assignments in late. After a couple of difficult weeks, I discovered that managing the all-nighters at the paper was simply a matter of budgeting my time. I finished my reading the weekend before it was due and completed all of my assignments early in the week. If I had a project due on a Friday, I made sure to get it done well in advance. Because I stuck to my schedule, late nights at the newspaper office didn't sabotage either my academic responsibilities or my social life. In fact, I was more efficient and also found that I had more free time to spend with friends.

This story demonstrates the speaker's ability to set priorities, manage his time, and successfully juggle various facets of his academic and personal life.

Decision Making

Decisive action taking is important to any business, whether your job involves working independently or in a group, but how you arrive at decisions will be of special interest to a prospective employer. Decision making involves generating multiple solutions to a problem and using your discernment to select the best choice from those options. Being judicious—thoughtfully weighing the pros and cons of a situation before taking action—is just as important as knowing how to make decisions. It involves deciphering which path to take and following a logical thought process to the end. If you've ever worked in student government or run a college organization, then you should have plenty of stories to tell about active decision making. Or, you could discuss how you chose your major, why you decided to take a certain class, or why you decided to attend your college. We make decisions every day, and any number of them could be incorporated into an anecdote to tell your interviewer. Try a college-related story like this one:

At my college, students typically live on campus for the first two years, and then they tend to find off-campus housing for the next two years. At the end of my sophomore year, I had to decide where to live in the fall, and with whom I wanted to share housing. My current roommate got offered a position as Resident Advisor on campus. The perks included a large room to share; the downside was that I'd have to remain on campus if I wanted to be her roommate. My other choices were to take a shared room in my sorority's house or take a private room in an apartment with three other friends, fellow education majors. The choices were tough: continuing to live with the "tried and true" roommate in a less-than-choice setting, giving up privacy for the potential fun that the sorority house offered, or taking the open room at the apartment, which was further from campus, but offered some personal space not often found at college. I opted for the apartment. I was scheduled for student-teaching the following spring semester, and

I knew that I'd need to go to bed early and prepare my lessons. I decided that the atmosphere at the sorority house could get tiring—if I wanted that scene, I could visit any time, day or night. I realized that I needed to be more independent, so the dorm option was out for me, too. I ended up making the right choice— I got my work done, had a successful experience in the classroom, and, with my own apartment, was able to invite my old roommate or sorority sisters over for an occasional escape from their surroundings.

Strategic Thinking

Thinking strategically is the ability to link long-range visions to daily work. The emphasis is on having a long-range goal where you needed to sustain effort over time despite setbacks and unpredictable events. In your academic experience, it could mean how you ensured that you graduated college in four years. In the workplace, it would translate to know the company initiative was to cut expenses, and the actions that you took to cut your expenses or save money for your department throughout the year. For example:

Midway through my sophomore year in college, I decided that I wanted to spend a semester studying in Paris. I was a French major, so I knew this would be the best way to improve my skills and knowledge of French culture. Some of my friends strongly advised against it, however—my college had a lot of course requirements, and many people who spent time abroad were unable to complete their degrees in four years or spent senior year struggling under impossible course loads. After thinking about the situation, I realized that studying abroad was not impossible—I just had to plan ahead. I had planned on taking two electives per semester, but I decided to replace one with a required course and add an additional required course to my schedule. Taking six courses a semester was tough, but I made a strict study schedule for myself and stuck to it. I studied in Paris during spring of my junior year, and it was the best educational experience I ever had. And, thanks to my good planning, I had no trouble completing my requirements. I was able to take all the electives I wanted senior year, and even had time to work as a research assistant for one of my French literature professors.

Staying Cool Under Pressure

Part of the maturity equation is coping with pressure, knowing what to do first when you walk into your office and have fifty e-mails and a ringing phone to answer—not to mention five people who are waiting for appointments. Think of a story about your own performance under pressure. Maybe you were on your college swim team and had a meet the day before a big test. Or maybe you came to work one day to discover that several employees were sick—and you were left to handle their work as well as your own. How did you control the situation? Was the result positive? Here's how Lance demonstrated his ability to handle pressure:

When dealing with pressure, I try to step back from situations and assess them logically, rather than getting carried away by my emotions. In college, I was the stage manager for the drama club's production of My Fair Lady. *When we got to the theater to pre-pare opening night, we discovered that all our props, makeup, and costumes were scattered and out of place. Apparently, a group of students had used the theater to practice some improvisational comedy, not knowing that a production was going up the next night. We didn't have much time to get ready, and the cast start-ed panicking about their missing items. I asked everyone to find his or her costume. While they were busy, I quickly found some cardboard boxes and labeled each one with a character's or group's name: Eliza, Henry, street merchants, racetrack patrons, and so on. The stage crew collected props and other items, brought them to me, and I deposited them in the proper box. Everything got sorted quickly, and the curtain went up on time.*

Rehearsing your stories

In order to weave your stories into an interview so that they sound effortless and natural, write them down and rehearse saying them several times. The goal is to be clear, concise, and to make your point; you don't want to sound like your answers are too pat or over-rehearsed. Eventually you may feel comfortable enough to tailor your stories to individual interviewers, but this takes a lot of practice. Recording your stories is a great way to hear all the things that need to be smoothed out or tightened so that your delivery is perfectly natural. Ask your family and friends to critique your stories and edit them. The reason for rehearsing your stories out loud is that the way you *tell* a story is very different from the way you write one.

While you're rehearsing, you may want to watch your facial expressions in a mirror. Are you smiling and enthused, or do you look overly somber and serious? Observe how your facial expressions affect your tone. When you're smiling, your voice sounds friendly, pleasing, and warm; when your expression is somber, your delivery may sound flat. Vary the tone of your voice and the tempo at which you speak. This will help create interest in what you are saying, especially if your interviewer's attention seems to be drifting away momentarily.

The point of rehearsing your stories isn't to memorize them. What you want is to become so familiar with them that you can hit the main point of each of your success stories even though you may not tell them exactly the same way every time. Relax, improvise, enjoy, and above all, feel confident about telling your stories. Just make sure you have stories for each success factor.

Because you can't possibly anticipate what the interviewer will ask, be prepared with several stories. For instance, you may have a great "problem solving" story, but unless you can engineer a smooth transition to it, chances are you'll have to rely on another story that can be worked into the conversation with more ease. Having lots of stories to draw on will give you the flexibility to react quickly to unexpected questions and shifts in conversation.

Being Honest

At this point you may be wondering if so much rehearsing is too much. Will all of this preparation, anticipation and planning make you seem less authentic—less like yourself? Of course you want to be truthful and act naturally at all times, but don't forget that an interview is just like any business meeting. Preparation is the key to getting your ideas across and facilitating a positive result.

To do well in an interview, you need to familiarize yourself completely with the sorts of questions you might be asked and rehearse your replies. It will help you to stay calm in a situation where there will be a raft of variables you can't control. For example, you will have no idea, beforehand, what your interviewer's body language will be like. While you're busy trying to "read" it, you'll be concentrating on making your own body language look positive. At the same time, you will be listening to your interviewer's questions, deciphering them, and forming a response. This can get tricky, so give yourself a break! Being prepared will give you a cushion on which to relax, and it'll make you feel more confident, too.

TYING INTERVIEWERS' QUESTIONS TO SUCCESS STORIES

So there's a lot going on the during the interview—you're listening to the question, trying to pick the right success story, watching the interviewer's nonverbal cues, and so on. The trick is to quickly pick out what the interviewer is asking you and then link the question to your success story.

Try this exercise. On the left hand of the column we've listed a typical interview question. On the right side, are suggestions for the success story topic. Cover the right hand column, and see if you can identify which of your success stories you would use to answer the question.

INTERVIEW QUESTION	SUCCESS STORIES
Give an example of a time when you worked on a team. What did you learn?	Teamwork or Team Leadership
Describe a challenging problem you had to solve and explain how you came up with your solution.	Innovative Thinking or Problem Solving
Have you ever had a conflict with a boss or a professor? How did you resolve it?	Communication or Problem Solving
What are your long-term career goals?	Strategic Thinking
What are you proudest of accomplishing?	Achievement/Getting Results
Were you ever in a position to have someone or some system impact your work negatively? What did you do?	Initiative
Did you ever make a decision that negatively affected someone else? What was the decision and what did you do about it?	Decision Making
Think of a time when you had to accomplish something under tight deadlines. What did you do? How did you handle it?	Staying Cool Under Pressure

THINGS TO DO THE DAY BEFORE AN INTERVIEW

- **Organize your clothing**
- **Make extra copies of your resume**
- **Make copies of your list of references**
- **Make a list of the questions you want to ask the interviewer**

- Write down the exact location of the interview, including the phone number
- Rehearse your success stories
- Plan how you will get to the interview, and map out an alternative route, just in case
- Pack a pen and paper
- Set your alarm clock
- Get a good night's sleep
- Plan to arrive 15 minutes early
- Remember the name of your interviewer
- Relax
- Feel confident
- Visualize success

....

PRESENTING YOURSELF

Before the interview, give yourself a little pep talk. Remember that there is a point to an interview, and that you have an objective. Remind yourself of what that objective is and visualize what success looks like to you. An interview is like a sales pitch, so before you go, tell yourself to be confident, that you're well prepared, enthusiastic, upbeat, and completely focused on your objective. Of course, there will always be some aspects of interviewing that are unpredictable. But you've probably had to think on your feet many times. Try to think of the interview as a learning experience. At the end of each interview, ask yourself, "What went well? What would I do differently?" If you can incorporate what you've learned into your next interview, you've been successful.

NONVERBAL CUES

Knowing how to read—and send—nonverbal cues can be extremely helpful in a situation where both interviewer and interviewee need to learn as much about each other as possible in a very short period of time. You certainly don't want to send the wrong message to an interviewer, so take the time to familiarize yourself with some of the more commonly used nonverbal cues.

There are dozens of them! But don't worry, you can think about and even practice most of them before going to an interview. An excellent way of seeing what some of your unconscious habits are is to ask a friend to videotape a rehearsed interview. It doesn't have to take long, and the family video-cam will do the trick. It is astonishing how unaware most of us are of our personal habits, posture, and gestures. Now is good a time to become familiar with them and make a few conscious changes. Here are some of the most common nonverbal cues to be aware of:

- Your handshake should be firm but not crushing
- Stand when you are being greeted or if you are greeting someone
- Look at your interviewer directly; make eye contact
- Smile or keep a pleasant expression on your face
- Avoid extraneous, nervous movements such as:
  Pushing your hair back
  Cupping your face in your hand and leaning your elbows on the table
  Tapping your foot
  Playing with your pen or pencil
  Tugging at your clothing
  Fidgeting
  Repeatedly touching your throat or mouth
- Do not slump in the chair or look down at your feet
- Keep your head up
- Keep both feet on the floor while seated; crossing your legs is acceptable (if this position makes you feel more relaxed)
- Keep your body relaxed
- Lean forward slightly to communicate that you are being attentive or move your chair forward as soon as the conversation starts

- Don't crowd your interviewer by sitting too close to him; respect his personal space
- Nod affirmatively to indicate that you understand a point, but do not overdo it
- Be aware of your posture: Don't cross or fold your arms. This is sometimes perceived as "defensive" or "protective"

The most important thing is to maintain normal eye contact with your interviewer, because it will show her that you are listening actively and interested in what she is saying. Be careful not to stare or you will likely make the interviewer feel uncomfortable. One technique you might use to practice looking directly at your interviewer without staring is to pretend that there is a triangle connecting the interviewer's right eye, left eye, and mouth. Try to keep your gaze focused on this triangle, without letting it linger on one point for too long. It might also help to conduct a practice interview with a friend and ask him to tell you if you are staring or allowing your eyes to wander.

Some people try to mirror the interviewer's body language—his facial expressions and gestures. If you try this, remember to be as subtle and natural as possible. Ultimately, what you want to "mirror" is your interviewer's communication style and level of energy. If you are alert, sympathetic, and listen attentively you will put your interviewer at ease. As a result, *you* will relax, too, and both of you will feel more comfortable in each other's company.

VERBAL CUES

Verbal cues are much easier to "read" than subtle visual cues, but they do require that you listen carefully. Some people are very good at remembering names, for example, but others tend to forget a name as soon as they hear it—especially in a tense or unusual situation. A good way not to forget your interviewer's name is to listen for it, of course, and then repeat it. For example, if your interviewer introduces himself to you as John, and says, "It's nice to meet you," your reply could be, "It's very nice to meet you, too, John." Once you've heard yourself actually say the name out loud it is much easier to remember it.

Good listening and speaking skills are essential to good interviewing because you always have to have one ear on the conversation while you plan your next comment or question. You certainly don't want to be so anxious about telling your own stories that you can't hear what the interviewer is saying. Consider the following story:

> Russell was incredibly nervous on the day of his interview with a major bank. He didn't want to stumble over his words, so he rehearsed his anecdotes over and over in his head. Unfortunately, he was rehearsing while his interviewer was talking to him about a recent change in corporate policy. When she asked him a question about the policy, Russell didn't know what to say—he hadn't heard a word of her explanation! It was obvious to the interviewer that Russell hadn't been paying attention.

Don't let this happen to you.

THE IMPORTANCE OF LISTENING

There are three good reasons for listening well:

1. To gain information about the job
2. To ask questions
3. To link what you have heard with the success story you want to tell

Summarizing information and using it to preface a question makes it clear to the interviewer that you've been listening and understand the information correctly, but it also gives you the opportunity to connect what you've just learned to an anecdote about yourself. For example, the interviewer has just told you that the company's objective for the year is to develop new business in a particular area and, consequently, certain departments will be reorganized or perhaps created in order to meet the new objective. You could start your response by summarizing: "Because the company is interested in new business development, I'm sure you're looking for people with initiative and creativity." This is your "in"—the appropriate moment to launch into one of your success stories. In this case, of course, the main idea would be to give a compelling example of your initiative.

....

Above all, remember that an interview is a conversation. Make sure that you are an active participant in that conversation.

....

Effective listening involves skill. Here are a few points about listening to keep in mind for an interview:

- Be attentive and lean forward slightly to signal that you are interested in what is being said
- Look directly at your interviewer, but in a *natural* way (without staring or blinking)
- Pay attention and stay in the present
- Don't interrupt
- Balance talking with listening
- Ask questions if there is something you don't understand, or if a point needs to be clarified
- Take the time to answer a question, rather than rushing in with a half-baked response

TALKING

In an interview, you will be doing a lot of talking, whether you're asking questions or responding to questions. In any case, you should be clear on your objectives: Why are you talking in this interview?

1. To give information
2. To sell yourself through your success stories
3. To project confidence
4. To demonstrate your communication skills

By showing that you are a good *listener*, you get more than information and an "in" to tell one of your success stories: listening makes a connection, establishes a rapport between you and the interviewer. The same applies to *talking*—to what you say. This requires a few good verbal communication skills. Here are a few basic tips:

- Be clear and concise. If your interviewer's attention seems to wander, you might be rambling. If he constantly has to ask you to say more about a question you just answered, you may not be saying enough.
- Make sure you have answered the question being asked.
- Be direct: Make declarative statements by using the word "I."
- Don't hedge: Avoid words and phrases such as "maybe," "perhaps," "you know," etc.
- Project your voice, so you can be heard clearly (but don't shout).
- Speak with enthusiasm.

If you are extroverted and social and tend to talk a lot (or perhaps even too much, on occasion), you will want to pull back in an interview. Pare down the stories you want to tell by eliminating extraneous information. Even better, conduct more practice interviews with friends and family; they can tell you if you are being overly gregarious. On the other hand, if you are quiet by nature, you will need to make an effort to become more actively engaged in the conversation and use more energy. This is where videotaping and rehearsing your success stories *before* an interview comes in handy. Listen to your stories again and again and cut or embellish them as you go along. Be sure to get as much critical input as you can from people you know, especially those who have been interviewed themselves or, even better, who have interviewed others.

PROOF OF CLAIM

The interview is a sales meeting, and your goal is to "sell yourself. " It's tempting to make flat assertions that you expect the interviewer to take on face value. Some of these assertions might be: "I'm a great worker, I'm punctual, upbeat, and diligent." The problem is that you are telling the interviewer what to think rather than proving your claim. By now, you've probably realized that this is what success stories are all about—backing up your claims about your abilities by giving a real-life example. So, if you're tempted to say that you're a good worker, then you need to give an example to back up that claim.

Often companies are looking for your experiences on a team and how you contributed to the overall team outcomes. So another thing to consider is when to say "I" and when to say "we." The answer is that you really have to balance both. It's a mistake to always say "we." The interviewer will never fully understand your individual contribution. In addition, if you always say "I," it will seem as if you weren't able to collaborate. A final word of caution: Don't be tempted to fabricate your role on a team. Company recruiters say that they are often in situations on campus where they interview every member of a team. Eventually, the real contributors to the team are clear to the recruiters because all the other team members corroborate their story.

• •

SELLING YOURSELF:
GOOD STORYTELLERS VS. BAD STORYTELLERS

Emily and Shira are both interviewing at an insurance company. The interviewer asks, "What are your strengths and weaknesses?"

Emily: **I'm a great worker. I'm punctual, efficient, upbeat, and diligent. These skills make me a perfect candidate for this job. I've never missed a deadline. I never received a word of negative feedback at my old job. My only real weakness is that I'm such a perfectionist.**

Shira: **My greatest strength is persistence. In my old job, I was on the audit team of a major cosmetics company. The team leader always gave me the fact-finding missions that had stumped everyone else. However, I sometimes try to take on too many projects at once, and it's difficult for me to admit that I can't handle my workload. I had to learn that there are times when the best thing to do is delegate tasks to other people.**

In this example, Emily is only giving flat assertion with no proof of claim. Shira, on the other hand, describes her strengths. She readily admits her faults, but also shows how she tries to overcome them.

The objective of any interview is to strike a balance between describing your accomplishments to the best of your ability and giving the interviewer enough room to judge them independently. In other words, don't try to tell the interviewer what to think. But *do* tell your stories as compellingly as possible. The power of influence should be wielded gently and used intelligently.

DRESS

Listening and responding well to your interviewer and subtly reflecting her body language, mood, and communication style will exert a powerful influence on how you are perceived by the interviewer. A rich mix of verbal and visual signals will pass between you, many of them on a subliminal level. But there is one aspect of interviewing that you can influence quite consciously through a nonverbal cue: clothing.

An entire lexicon has been written on the subject of "dressing for success," but perhaps the best approach is to keep it simple. For example, why not put together a couple of interview "uniforms" that look great and make you *feel* great every time you wear them. For the sake of saving time and anxiety (not to mention money), it helps to have fewer choices. If you want to refresh the look of your "uniform," you can always accessorize.

• •

If you are a woman, keep your dresser well stocked with pantyhose. You don't want to wake up on the morning of an interview to discover that every pair of stockings you own is either in the laundry basket or full of runs! And be sure to tuck a pair into your purse or briefcase—if you get a run on the way to the interview, you'll be prepared.

Men should pay careful attention to details. Shined shoes will make you look professional and polished. If you have facial hair, be sure it's trimmed and neat. Your tie should be simple and appropriate—you don't want to show up at an interview with a conservative bank wearing a loud or garish tie.

• •

Looking professional

The main point about dressing for an interview is to feel that the clothes you are wearing are both comfortable and appropriate. In most cases "appropriate" means "professional." Of course, there are many ways to interpret what professional is, but if you don't know, ask someone whose authority you trust.

Your best bet is to go with a business suit. A suit always looks professional and shows that you are serious about finding a good job. Your suit should be well-tailored and dark in color—stick with black, dark gray, navy blue, or dark brown. Shoes should be clean and polished, and accessories should be conservative. You don't want to show up in a nice business suit with a neon green watch on your wrist. Make sure that your hair is neat and combed and that your shoes aren't scuffed or dirty.

If you are a woman, stick with small earrings and simple necklaces, such as a strand of pearls or a gold chain. Keep your makeup simple and conservative. If you decide to wear a skirt, make sure that it is an appropriate length. Generally, skirts should be no shorter than an inch or two above the knee.

Some small or creative companies may not mind if you dress down for an interview. For men, this usually means slacks with a jacket and tie. A woman might wear dress pants or a skirt with a blouse or sweater set. Again, you should try to keep accessories to a minimum and avoid loud colors. But only choose one of these more casual options if you are *sure* that it is appropriate. You might be making a big mistake if you assume that a particular company will be relaxed about what you wear to the interview. The employees at a particular firm might wear jeans, but that doesn't mean that you should wear jeans to your interview—you're not an employee yet.

In addition to looking professional, you also want to be comfortable. Make sure that your clothing fits properly. You don't want to spend the entire interview squirming in a pair of pants that are too tight. Also make sure that your clothing is weather-appropriate. If you're interviewing at an Arizona law firm in the middle of August, you don't want to be wearing a wool suit. Iron your clothing the night before the interview, so that you can be unhurried and relaxed the next day.

If you're not sure what to wear, ask. If you know someone at the firm with which you're interviewing, he or she will give you the best information. You can also ask someone in the same industry. Dress codes may vary widely in different industries. If you can't think of anyone to ask, call the human resources department and explain that you need some guidance. Or, go to your college career center for advice.

WHAT DID YOU WEAR TO YOUR INTERVIEW?

- "I wore a charcoal gray suit with a white shirt, and had my dress shoes shined the day before the interview. My tie added a little color, but it wasn't loud. I opted to bring a leather portfolio instead of a briefcase. If you're still in college, I think it sometimes looks a little silly if you carry a briefcase. The interviewer knows that you don't use it regularly, so it seems more like a prop."

—MIKE, MANAGEMENT CONSULTANT

- "I wore a black business suit with a lavender silk shirt, black stockings, and black pumps. I accessorized with pearl earrings and a pearl necklace. I usually don't wear cosmetics, but because I look very young, I wore some simple, natural-looking makeup."

—ANASTASIA, PARALEGAL

- "I wore a black suit with a blue button-down shirt and low-heeled shoes. I also wore a simple gold necklace and small, gold earrings. My office is pretty casual, but I wanted to make a good first impression. After I was hired, I was able to get more creative about the way I dress."

—PEGGY, EDITORIAL ASSISTANT

The way you dress should tell a story that is compatible both with who you are and what is required for the job. Moreover, if you feel comfortable in your clothes you will feel more confident about yourself in general.

BEFORE YOU LEAVE THE INTERVIEW

The way you say good-bye is just as important as the way you greet an interviewer. As you leave, try to maintain the same level of enthusiasm, interest, and sincerity you brought to the interview. Above all, be *tactful* as you make your exit, even if you feel that the interview didn't go as smoothly or as positively as you had hoped it would. You should thank your interviewer for having taken the time to speak with you and answer your questions ("It's been a pleasure meeting you and your associates"). Express interest in the job ("I'm very interested in the job and would really enjoy working with your team"). And ask what the next step is ("May I phone your office in a few days to find out about your decision, or would you prefer that I contact your human resources department for further information?"), and don't leave the interview until you know.

AFTER THE INTERVIEW

Whew, you made it! You have earned the right to relax as soon as you get home. Peel off those pantyhose and whip off that suit jacket! After you've given yourself plenty of time to come down from the interview, take some time to think about what happened. While it's still fresh in your mind, replay the interview and put yourself in the interviewer's shoes. How do you think you came off? What can you learn from analyzing your "performance," and how will it help you at the next interview?

How did I do?

To help you organize your thoughts, write them down on a piece of paper or in a journal or diary (if you keep one). If you took notes during the interview or immediately afterward, read them now. Make a list of things you can do to present yourself a little differently at the next interview. A sample list might look like this:

- Stay focused on the current question, and don't worry about previous answers

- Do more research on the company so you can ask more questions
- Practice the success story on taking initiative
- Wear something more comfortable
- Try to relax (do deep breathing exercises before the interview)
- Smile more
- Wake up 30 minutes earlier to allow for more prep time
- Bring paper to take notes

Evaluating the company

Interviewing is a two-way process: While the interviewer is assessing you, you are evaluating whether this is the best position and company for you. Will it allow you to use your skills, learn, and excel? The chart you made in Chapter 3 ("Ten Requirements for the Ideal Job") will help you analyze your prospective employer. Take a look at your list of requirements. How does the company stack up against your criteria? Did you get all the information you wanted to know about the company from the interviewer? What questions could you ask next time to find out more? Review the list carefully before the next interview. If you think you might forget some questions, bring the list with you.

Now, think about the person who would be your boss. Did you get a good feeling from her? If you didn't "click" instantly or if you can't quite make up your mind about how you'd feel if she became your boss:

- Make a list of desirable and less desirable characteristics for an employer to have. Check your interviewer against it. How does she rate?
- Ask yourself if you could learn from her. If so, what would she teach you?
- Think about the questions you can ask the next time to find out if your prospective employer is the right boss for you.

Saying Thank You

The next step to take after you come home from an interview is to write a thank-you note. Be aware that notes of this kind are meant to be more than polite. In fact, they are powerful selling tools, so write them carefully. Your thank-you note should show appreciation for the time the interviewer took with you *and* reinforce that you are the ideal candidate.

Even though some people might believe that writing a thank-you note is optional, it is not. As the formal conclusion to an interview, a thank-you note is *required*. Think of it as an essential feature of your job application. To write one of these important notes as effectively as possible, make sure that you address the following points:

- Tell the interviewer how much you enjoyed meeting her (and her staff)
- Express your enthusiasm for the job and the company
- Repeat the main reason why you think you're the best candidate for the job
- Clarify or state an important point that you might have fumbled or forgotten about during the interview
- Establish when the next contact will be, unless you feel more comfortable with a closing statement such as "thank you for your time" and/or "I look forward to hearing from you."

Although it is generally agreed that a thank-you note should be short, opinions differ as to whether it should be handwritten or typed. It is safe to say, however, that if a company is conservative, the best bet would be to write your thanks by hand on a small, plain, good-quality note card (5″ x 3½″). On the other hand, you can type your thanks on good-quality, standard size (8½″ by 11″) stationery. Some job candidates use the same paper and style of heading they used for their resumes and cover letters. (In this instance, the thank-you note is considered the final addition to the resume package they've already submitted.) The format is less important than the

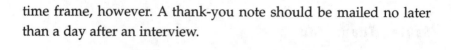

time frame, however. A thank-you note should be mailed no later than a day after an interview.

* * *

Don't underestimate the power of a thank-you note. When two equally qualified candidates are under consideration, deciding whom to choose often comes down to who is the most courteous. Make sure that person is you.

* * *

If you opt to send thank-you cards, go to your local stationery store and buy a box of good quality cards and keep them on hand for other interviews. Don't forget to send a thank-you note to everyone you met at the interview, including the person who took you from one interview (or interviewer) to the next. If you're not quite sure how to write a thank-you note, take a look at the sample on the next page. More sample letters are included in Appendix D.

Following up

If you haven't heard from your interviewer or human resources contact by the appointed time, follow up with a call of your own or send an e-mail. A good way to re-open the conversation with your contact in human resources, or with the interviewer, is to call back a few days after the interview and ask if you can clarify or add to any of the answers you gave during the interview.

Being prepared with many detailed success stories and anecdotes will ensure a successful interview. At the same time, don't forget to be aware: listen carefully to the interviewer; notice your body language (and his); and be conscious of your speech patterns. Use your best communication skills and demonstrate your awareness by asking questions. Not only will this action show that you have been paying attention, it will help ensure that both you and the company are a good match. Be sure to dress the part for the job you want;

Veronica Carruthers
10 Seagull Lane • Madison, CT 01888 • 402-555-3821

June 7, 2000

Ms. Brenda Jones
East Harbor Research Lab
114 East Harbor Road
Mystic, CT 01842

Dear Ms. Jones:

I wanted to thank you again for meeting with me yesterday. I very much enjoyed speaking with you and your staff, and I am very excited about the possibility of working for East Harbor Research Lab. I am confident that my background in chemistry and my research experience and the Park Science Center would make me an asset to the lab.

Please don't hesitate to call me if you have any further questions. I will contact you next week to discuss the next step in the interview process.

Thank you for your time and consideration.

Sincerely,

Veronica Carruthers

make sure that you look neat, capable, and professional. Finally, don't forget to write a thank-you note to your interviewer. This step is both a courtesy and a smart way to follow-up because it serves as a reminder that you are willing and able to be a great addition to the company.

WHAT QUESTIONS SHOULD YOU ASK?

You've already given yourself a tremendous advantage if you've taken the time to research the company that is giving you an interview. (Please see Chapter 3 for more information.) Your questions will be all the more informed and your interviewer will be impressed with your resourcefulness. If you've listened well during the interview and have garnered new information, take the opportunity to use it as a frame for your next question (as suggested earlier in this chapter). Or use a fact you already know to ask more questions about the company. When you are preparing questions, either before or during the interview, make sure you ask:

- Questions about the job
- Questions about the company

This seems fairly obvious, but sometimes people are so focused on getting a job and understanding what the expectations of that specific job are that they lose track of the bigger picture. This omission will give your interviewer information about you that you might not have counted on. You don't want people to think that you're mono-focused. But over and above that you probably *do* want to know what other people in the company are doing and what the corporate goal or direction is. Ask what projects you'll work on if you get the job.

Pearl of Wisdom

DON'T LET YOUR MIND WANDER.

"I interviewed a candidate for an entry-level position at a telecommunications start-up. It became clear to me that he wasn't paying attention to me when I asked him, 'What does success mean to you?' and, after a long pause, during which he looked very confused, he answered, 'Salary can be variable depending on the availability of stock options, bonuses, etc. I'm sure you'll make me a fair offer based on what you see on my resume.' The moral of the story: You shouldn't let your mind wander during an interview, but if you do catch your mind drifting, it is much more professional to ask the interviewer to repeat the question than to take a stab in the dark."

—NICK, DIRECTOR OF TECHNOLOGY

CHAPTER 5

the interview

Your Success Stories in Action

PREPARING FOR A winning interview is all about knowing your strengths and being confident of your accomplishments. Already, you've mastered how to research a job, conduct yourself in an interview, construct effective success stories, and follow through after an interview has ended. Now, the combination of your resume and knowing your success stories should boost your confidence to the degree that you will go into any interview relaxed, energetic, and ready to talk about yourself—instead of feeling that you can hardly wait for it to be over.

However, before you go any further, it is essential to learn the mechanics of *various types* of interviews in order to do well in each of them. Although it is true that most interviews share the same basic expectations, there are a number of different interview formats and processes. For example, in a panel or group interview you will be expected to converse with and answer questions from several people over the course of a morning or an afternoon. Or you may be called upon to talk about yourself to a single recruiter during a five-minute campus interview. On the other hand, you may find yourself looking across a restaurant table at an interviewer, while you skillfully blend pleasantries with some of your better success stories.

This chapter provides a thorough understanding of informational and standard interviews and shows how to navigate them for maximum effect. Chapter 6 follows through with all the information, tips, and advice you'll need to anticipate every requirement and protocol of off-site, group, panel, and campus interviews, as well as case, recruiter, internal, and stage two interviews.

The first type of interview to be discussed in this chapter—the informational or networking interview—is different from the others because there may not be an actual job opening. Such interviews will help you research an industry, company, or job category. You will also be discussing your strengths and career aspirations in the hopes that industry professionals know of suitable contacts or open positions for you. In a standard interview, you will be required to ask and respond to questions. However, the objective of an informational interview is to illustrate the strength of your skills, the best qualities of your personality, and the breadth of your accomplishments. This chapter teaches you how to reach that objective through the judicious use of well-crafted anecdotes.

INFORMATIONAL INTERVIEWS

If you're a recent college graduate looking for your first job, you may not be entirely certain about the kind of work you want to do. You will undoubtedly have questions about certain fields or business and want information before you launch a job search. Of course, there are many options for researching jobs in the library and on the Internet. Your friends, family, and network are also extremely useful sources of general information and advice. But, if you want inside information, you'll need to set up an informational interview with someone who is *already* doing the work that you may be interested in doing. There are several advantages to this kind of interviewing:

1. You'll find out whether or not you want to go into a particular field.
2. In the process of gathering information and meeting people, you may be given leads about openings for jobs in the industry.
3. You may be referred to specific people at other companies for more information or perhaps job interviews.
4. You may be offered a job.
5. A job may be created for you.

The person you want to contact and meet for an informational interview should be in a position to hire. It's important to remember, however, that the primary objective of this kind of interview is to gather information—the likelihood of there being an open job on the day you come for your interview is slim. In addition, the person you are coming to see knows that the main objective of your conversation is to share information, not to "make a sale." Ideally, you will have obtained the name of this person from someone in your network, but if no one you know has a personal contact in the field that interests you, there are other options:

- Call an alumnus of your university who is in the field that interests you. Although you may not know him, you both share the common experience of attending the same university. Most alumni are very willing to help out recent graduates.
- Write a letter to the senior-level person you would like to meet. Refer to industry directories, either in the library or on the Internet, for names, titles, addresses, and phone numbers. Be sure to call the company to make sure she is still there and to find out if her title has changed. Your letter to her should be very clear about what you want. Here are some tips to follow:

1. Explain that you are researching a field (children's book publishing, for example), because you think it might be a career you'd be interested in pursuing.
2. Request a very short meeting for information gathering.
3. Briefly describe your background in terms of education and work experience (if you have any).
4. State that you will call in a few days to follow up.

When you make your follow-up call, you may be asked to speak with someone at a lower level in the company or with the human resources department. This is good news: When you call for an appointment, you can mention the name of the senior level person who referred you. Simply say something like, "I was referred by Eleanor Klein in the research and development department."

On the other hand, some executives and managers are reluctant to meet with people they don't know. Others are simply too busy to take the time for informational interviews. But if you do get through to someone who is willing to talk with you, refer to the letter you wrote and explain again that you would like to meet *briefly* to gather information and learn more about the field. You don't want to imply that you are looking for a job: You only want information.

What's it all about?

Some day you will receive a networking call from a person who wants 15 minutes of your time to learn more information about your company. How would you like to spend those 15 minutes? You'd want the person to be interesting, to ask about you, and to be prepared with thoughtful questions about your company and industry. That's the model.

There are three parts to an informational interview: talking about yourself, learning about your contact, and learning about your contact's company.

You could start out the interview by saying, "Thank you for agreeing to see me. It may be helpful for me to tell you a little bit about myself, and then I'd like to ask you how you got started in your career." At first, when talking about yourself, keep it short. Tell the contact briefly about your background, why you're interested in the field, and then weave in more information as the interview proceeds, looking for ways to link your experiences to what your contact is saying.

Once you've given your contact information about yourself, turn your focus on him and his company or industry. You'll want to maximize what you learn in a short period of time, so consider asking some of these questions:

- What are typical entry-level positions in this field?
- What role do you play in the company?
- How did you start out in your career?
- Do you wish you had done anything differently?
- What advice do you have for someone starting out in this field?
- I'm interested in the position of _____. Do you think I'm qualified for this job, or would you suggest that I receive more education or training?
- Are there any specific skills I should develop?
- What kind of job do you think I'm qualified for?
- What does the typical career path look like for a job of this kind?
- What makes an employee successful in this job/company?
- What are the mistakes that people in this field typically make?
- Is there anything new or particularly exciting that is happening or has happened in the field recently?
- What companies are your competitors? How does your company distinguish itself?
- What sort of future do you anticipate for this industry?
- Are there any trade magazines or other industry publications I should read for more information?
- Do you have any sense of what a first-year salary might look like?

- How quickly do people in this field advance?
- Is there anyone else in your company or in another company with whom I should speak about this job/field?

If you know something about the field, industry, or company under discussion, you will make a much stronger impression on your interviewer, as discussed in Chapter 3. Prepare for this interview as you would any other. Bring copies of your resume and make sure that your cover letter has given your interviewer a strong sense of your background and what it is you want to learn about the field. At the interview, take notes.

Where do we go from here?

There may be a number of outcomes from an informational interview:

- You get the information you want and you can add one person to your professional network.
- Your interviewer takes an active interest in you and suggests a second meeting.
- Your interviewer suggests that you meet one or more of her colleagues, who may be in a position to hire.

An important goal of informational interviews is to expand your network. Some experts say that you should leave an informational interview with at least three additional names to add to your network. It is important to take the initiative to ask your contact if she knows anyone else with whom you should speak, given your background and career objective. Remember to send a thank-you note to your contact and add her name to the list of people you will notify when you secure employment.

If you are fortunate, and your contact refers you to other people in the field, you may use her name when contacting them. You can either phone or write when setting up appointments, but be sure to mention the name of the person who referred you. Also, don't forget to mention what you're calling about. After each meeting, be sure to send a thank-you note. Even if the first person to give you an informational interview does not refer you to anyone else, have the courtesy and professionalism to send a thank-you note. (Review the samples in Chapter 4 and Appendix D.) At the very least, informational interviewing is an excellent way of getting firsthand knowledge and advice about various career options. At best, you may be offered a job or one may be created for you.

THE TRADITIONAL INTERVIEW

If you are going on a traditional (or "standard") interview with a small company, you will likely meet your interviewer right away. At a larger company, you might be asked to fill out an application in the human resources department first. You will have a copy of your resume handy, so you will be able to complete the application quickly and easily.

It is also common to meet with more than one person, especially at larger companies. You might meet with a human resources professional, and then speak with a supervisor. The interview with the person who will supervise you if you get the job will last longer than the other interviews. (Do remember, though, that there are no hard and fast rules, and interviewing methods vary widely from company to company.)

An interview with a human resources professional will be very different than an interview with a supervisor. This interview will determine whether or not you will be passed on to the hiring department. Part of this interview will be spent acquainting you with the company in general and the position in particular. You will also be asked some general questions about your skills and experiences. Although human resources personnel do not make final hiring decisions, they *are* asked for feedback about candidates. So be sure to use your success stories and treat this interview as seriously as you would any other.

Assuming that you've arrived on time, your primary interview with your potential supervisor will last thirty minutes to an hour. (Again, there are no hard and fast rules about interviews.) A longer interview should be interpreted as a good sign. But if you come and go in ten minutes, it's likely that something didn't work out—maybe you were the wrong fit, or perhaps the interviewer preferred another candidate.

If things continue to go well, your primary interviewer may ask you to speak to someone else (or several other people) as well, either right then or a little later in the day. This is another good sign. It usually means that your interviewer thinks you are a viable candidate for the job. You will get to know more about the company and hear different points of view. Sometimes, because of the necessity to fill positions quickly, especially in fast-paced growth sectors, you will meet with more than one person on the same day. If you are perceived as a highly qualified candidate by this kind of company, the interview process will be sped up to ensure that you don't get hired elsewhere. So, try to be flexible about time. Avoid scheduling interviews back to back and give yourself plenty of time between appointments to respond to unexpected developments.

The nuts and bolts

Most standard interviews generally begin in one of two scenarios: Your potential supervisor will start things off by asking you questions, or your potential supervisor will describe the job and then ask you questions. Scenario two is the most advantageous because you are given information before any questions are asked. This will give you plenty of time to decide which success story you'll use to illustrate one of your skills, strengths, or accomplishments. As you will remember from Chapter 4, each of your success stories should be built around one of the **Ten Success Factors** that most employers look for in job candidates:

- Accomplishments/Getting Results
- Taking Initiative

- Communication Skills
- Problem Solving
- Teamwork and Team Leadership
- Project Management
- Decision Making
- Strategic Thinking
- Innovative Thinking
- Handling Pressure

Telling success stories well is the most effective way to illustrate your accomplishments because it puts each one into a credible—and memorable—context. Long before you go to your first interview you will have written and rehearsed many success stories for each success factor listed above and you will be ready to weave them skillfully into your answers. (For more detailed information about success stories, please refer to Chapter 4.)

Yes or No

Keep in mind that if you start answering questions with a simple "yes" or "no," you're on the wrong track. Other one or two-word responses won't help you either. For example, if the interviewer asks what your best quality is and your response is "Analyzing things," you won't be telling the interviewer enough about yourself to understand how you think or the breadth of your experience. You need to share as much information about yourself as possible, so that your interview understands how you think and what your skills and qualifications are. Show off your interpersonal skills, personality, and even your sense of humor.

Success Story to the rescue

So, what should you do when your interview asks about your best quality? Tell a success story. For example, you might say:

One of the qualities I can really count on is my ability to analyze and resolve problems, particularly when people are in conflict. When I was in college, I was the Resident Advisor of my floor in the dorm. There were about twenty-four of us altogether, and I was often called on to arbitrate and settle arguments. It always seemed so clear to me what the answer was, maybe because I'm the oldest of four children in my family. One time, two women in the dorm couldn't agree over the use of the telephone—there was only one phone at our end of the hall—which meant that twelve of us were expected to share it. Anyway, one woman accused the other of monopolizing the phone. It seemed pretty clear to me that the only way to satisfy both women—and the rest of us, for that matter— would be to agree, as a group, how long each of us should stay on the phone at any given time. Once everyone knew what the "rule" was, there were far fewer conflicts.

Proof of Claim

When you answer a question with a story, such as the one above, you are giving the interviewer two things:

1. Information
2. Proof of claim

Anyone can say that he or she has good conflict management skills and leave it at that, but telling a success story that illustrates your point *proves* your claim. In the process, you are giving the interviewer other information, such as: You were in a position of leadership, understood it, and rose to the challenge. When there were conflicts in the dorm, you didn't just shut your door or walk away; you actually interceded, which took initiative. And, of course, you solved the problem. So, a simple question, such as "what's your best quality," can give you a valuable opportunity to give the interviewer a fuller picture of your capabilities.

MOST INTERVIEWS HAVE FIVE STAGES:

1. **Introductions.** No matter who you are meeting, whether it's someone from Human Resources or the person who might eventually be your boss, remember to shake hands, smile, and introduce yourself: "Hello, my name is Maria Sangenaro and I'm very pleased to meet you." Try to remember each interviewer's name by repeating it, writing it down, or asking for a business card.
2. **Small talk.** Casual conversation at the beginning of an interview puts everyone at ease and makes the transition to the next stage of the interview seem more natural and pleasant. A quick comment on the beautiful weather, the ease of your commute to the interview, or a positive observation about the office building are possible ice-breakers.
3. **Exchanging Information.** After you've introduced yourself and exchanged pleasantries, you will be expected to answer questions about your background and experience. This is when you will tell success stories in order to convey a strong sense of who you are and what you are capable of accomplishing. Don't forget to ask questions about the company and position.
4. **Summarizing.** There is a natural point in every interview where there are no more questions to ask. Summarize what you've heard about the responsibilities of the position. Clarify any information that was unclear.
5. **Closing the Interview.** Leave on a positive note: Make a

final statement about your interest in the job and the company. Find out what happens next. How will you know if a decision has been made? Before leaving make sure your interviewer has a copy of your resume and references, and ask for her card. Thank her for her time, smile, and shake her hand.

IT'S ALL ABOUT INFORMATION

No matter how you look at it, the heart of an interview is an exchange of information. *How* you convey information about yourself is what counts: This is why it is so vital to know and tell your success stories effectively.

As mentioned earlier, you can expect a standard interview to open with a question or with a description of the job and the company—and then a few questions. Of course, you will be called upon to ask a few questions of your own, but any variation of scenarios will give you ample opportunity to use your success stories. If you have a good interviewer who asks open-ended questions, you will be able to tell your stories with that much more facility.

Every interview is different, as you might expect, so you can't predict all the questions an interviewer will ask; because your answers will prompt follow-up questions, the interviewer will likely ask a number of questions that even *he* didn't know he would ask. Some interviewers might begin with questions about your educational background or previous work experiences to determine if you have the skills or training for a particular job, while others may ask more general questions about your motivations, goals, accomplishments and ambitions. If you've worked previously, your interviewer may want to know why you left your last job, how long you were there, and what your position and salary were, etc. If you did not go to or finish college, you may be asked questions about why you do not have a degree. If you do have a college degree, you might be asked how you selected your major, what you did during your summers, or how college has prepared you for the job.

Finding an approach

Whatever the question, just do your best to answer it completely. Bear in mind that the interviewer's main objective is to determine whether you are the right person for the job. Your objective is twofold:

- To answer your interviewer's questions as completely as possible
- To convince your interviewer that you are the right choice for the job

The best way to achieve your objective is to use your success stories. Going into an interview, you know that you have at least ten ways to talk about your accomplishments. When asked a question, focus on its meaning. There's usually a word or two in the question, such as "accomplishments," "goals," or "team," that will help you determine which success story is most appropriate. Chapter 7 presents some of the tough questions you might be asked; be sure to take a look at them in order to be better prepared for unexpected or particularly thorny questions. Meanwhile, the following list will help you anticipate **some of the questions that are most frequently asked:**

- How would you describe yourself?
- What are your strengths?
- What are your weaknesses?
- What are your goals for the next year?
- What is your greatest accomplishment?

Making a connection

You may have noticed that there is some crossover between the questions in the list above and the Ten Success Factors that were listed earlier in this chapter.

In fact, the Ten Success Factors are simply a short list of the qualities most employers look for in job applicants. And, as you'll recall, each of your success stories should be built around one of the Ten Success Factors. Any of the questions in the long list above, however, will help you prepare your stories. Read the list carefully and think of the experiences you've had that might illustrate your communication skills, for example, or your ability to manage pressure or make difficult decisions. The main objective is to link your special qualities, abilities, and successes to the questions interviewers ask you.

Tell me a story

Although you could certainly answer a question such as "How would you describe yourself?" with a few well-chosen words, you wouldn't be telling your interviewer enough about your strengths and abilities. However, if you approach these questions a little differently and link them to one of your success factors such as "initiative" or "problem solving" you would do a far better job of both answering the questions and creating a convincing image of your potential. Now is the time to tell a story. Here's an example of how you can do it:

Question: How would you describe yourself?
Answer: I'm a self-motivated person who is very goal-oriented. In my junior year of college, I knew that I wanted an internship at a consulting firm. One of my friends who was a senior told me that a certain firm really valued her experience as president of the campus geology club. Since I was a business and accounting major, I ran for treasurer of Future Leaders of America. I gained

valuable experience in keeping financial records, and also got to head our first fund-raiser. What a great experience and, as you can see from my resume, I did get to work for that consulting firm.

This success story doesn't take more than a minute to tell, but look at *how much* it says about your financial savvy, innovative thinking, and ability to:

- Lead others
- Make decisions
- Set and meet important goals
- Self-motivate
- Solve problems
- Communicate well

This story shows off many success factors, and gives you the opportunity to share something personal, but not private. This applicant has shown that he has a healthy dose of self-esteem, too. He's highlighted his leadership skills as well as his technical skills. Remember, the interviewer can read facts about you straight from your resume. The interview is all about conveying your credentials and communicating the hows and the whys of your experience in a cohesive narrative form.

Another story

Even though you might be able to comfortably tell a success story in about one minute, you may not always have the time to tell as many as you'd like. Ideally, you want to tell ten stories that illustrate ten success factors over the course of an interview. But in the real world, interviews are sometimes cut short. Or perhaps the interviewer simply doesn't provide you with enough opportunities to insert more than a few stories. However, you should try to illustrate as many success factors as possible. Therefore, try to write and rehearse stories that demonstrate more than one success factor. The previous story is a good example. Here's another sample:

Question: How do you handle pressure?

Answer: My internship at TLS Advertising involved a lot of pressure. I was working for an account executive who was responsible for the firm's cosmetics clients. We had strict deadlines and were often juggling more than one project at a time. One of my jobs was to help my boss prepare for client pitches and sales calls. In the process of creating all the overheads and ancillary materials she needed, I worked with the art department. I had to figure out how to make our project their top priority when they had so many competing demands. The art department depended on timely, clear communication, and I did my best to accommodate them. I set up time and action calendars and would talk to them hourly when necessary. In fact, I kept in such close contact with that department, that they came to rely on my trafficking skills, which they asked me to demonstrate to the other departments so that their workflow could be managed more efficiently.

The narrator of this success story managed to weave in at least four success factors—each one a highly desirable, marketable skill such as:

- Handling Pressure
- Taking Initiative
- Team Work
- Problem Solving

A short story

There may be times when you want to emphasize a single success factor: perhaps you want to call attention to a certain skill, or maybe you are running low on time but want to squeeze in one last example. Here's an example:

Question: Would you say you're a team player?

Answer: I've been very involved in sports at college. I played on the baseball and basketball teams, and participated in a number of intramural sports. Last year, our basketball team won the regional championships. We had to compete against eleven other teams. The competition was grueling. We had excellent coaching, but what really won the day for us was our ability to pull together as a team. We discovered that we each had individual strengths and could learn a lot from each other. For me, that meant learning to pass more often, instead of always taking a shot.

Of course, this story *does* point out more than the speaker's ability to work on a team. For example, it gives you a sense of her personal tenacity and her ability to handle pressure well and learn from her mistakes. The possibilities for good storytelling are endless. The trick is to know your experiences, skills, and personal qualities *so well* that you can adapt them to almost *any* question or questioning style.

Most importantly, don't forget to enjoy the interview. Nowhere is it written in stone that an interview *has to be* cheerless, tense, confrontational, frightening, or boring. Make your stories as interesting as possible—they'll invite questions and responses from your interviewer that will open up the conversation even more.

IT'S A TWO-WAY CONNECTION

The more you and your interviewer know about each other, the easier it will be to determine whether or not you are a good fit for the job. You won't know, however, until you've asked a few questions of your own. Go into an interview with the attitude that you are there to learn about a job, instead of feeling overwhelmed by the idea that you there to be judged. If you take an investigative, proactive approach, you won't worry as much about your "performance" or nervously wait for the next baited question to catch you off-guard. If you concentrate on finding out about your interviewer and the company, your energies and attention will be directed *outward* instead of *inward*. This will make you feel more in control and, consequently, less nervous. Don't approach your interviewer as an adversary; it will only make your questions sound inquisitorial, instead of friendly and interested. If you've prepared your questions ahead of time you'll feel even more confident and ready to learn.

What questions should you ask?

You've already given yourself a tremendous advantage if you've taken the time to research the company (please see Chapter 3 for details). Your interviewer will be favorably impressed if your questions demonstrate knowledge of the company's history, successes, goals, and plans. You might ask about recent events at the company. For instance, you could ask a recruiter at a law firm: "I read recently that your firm is involved in a major lawsuit regarding patent violations. I'm very interested in intellectual property law. Is this something this firm specializes in?" Or, if you're interviewing at a small publishing company, you might say, "I noticed that you recently published a book on childcare, although most of your previous publications were novels. Is this a new direction you're going in?" But if you ask questions such as "What business is your company in?" or "What are your firm's services?" you'll convey how little effort and thought you've put into the interview. Asking good questions, on the other hand, isn't about showing off. You obviously want to know as much as you can about a company if you're seriously interested in accepting the job (should it be offered to you). And there are some intangible things about a company that are hard to find in the public record, such as information about corporate culture. So, when you are preparing questions either before or during the interview, make sure you consider asking some of these questions.

Questions to ask about the company:

- Does the company promote a certain philosophy?
- What is the corporate vision or mission?
- Does the company promote people from within?
- What is it like to work in the company?
- What do employees like about working for the company? What don't they like?
- Who are the people who have been the most successful in the company? What were—or are—their personality traits and characteristics? What do they have in common?
- Does the company have plans for expansion?
- Where is the most growth in the company?
- What is the company's position regarding the industry in general?
- What is the firm's competition?
- What are some of the most important projects the company is involved in at the moment?
- Are there any new products or services?

Ask as many questions as you need to get a complete picture of the job and the company. Again, both you and the interviewer want to be sure of each other. You both have essentially the same goal: to determine whether or not you want to continue your relationship. Your interviewer wants to find out if she should invite you back for a second interview, and you want to find out if the company should stay on your list of choice employers. Make sure you space your questions throughout the interview, so you don't have a long list at the end, and give your interviewer plenty of time to answer. Don't barrage her with questions.

....

WHAT YOU SHOULDN'T ASK

Depending on the company, you will have a short meeting with a human resources officer either before or after your interview. In any case, she should be able to answer all your questions about:

- Salary
- Benefits
- Vacations

Although your interviewer may tell you about some of the company's benefits, she may not know or remember all the specifics about taxes, health insurance, dental plans, profit sharing, retirement compensation, unemployment compensation, sick days, family leave, or vacations. If she is unable to give you information you need, ask for another contact in the company. Wait to discuss salary with your interviewer until she mentions it first. Human resources will give you all the details if your interviewer does not.

....

Advertisements for yourself

If you don't ask questions, your interviewer will assume that you're not interested in the company—or the job. Moreover, you won't be able to make an informed decision about the job, should it be offered to you, if you don't ask questions. There are other good reasons for asking questions:

1. Asking questions demonstrates the value you place on work and your career
2. Asking questions demonstrates your depth of knowledge about the field

3. Asking questions gives you more opportunities to "sell" yourself to a potential employer

Just as you were prompted by your interviewer's questions to talk about your accomplishments, the questions you ask your interviewer will reveal information that you can use to further exhibit your skills and qualification for the job. In other words, if you use questions to discover what the needs of your prospective employer are, you can use your success stories, once again, to illustrate how you can satisfy those needs. Your success stories are the best proof of your accomplishments. And, as we all know, "past performance is the best indicator of future performance."

Relating your success stories to the job

If you've arrived at the interview having researched the company, you probably have a relatively good sense of how well the company is doing, what its goals are, and in which direction it is growing. During the interview, listen to what your interviewer says about what the company needs and look for an opportunity to interject an advertisement for yourself. For example, a scenario might play this way:

You: Where is the most growth in the company?

Interviewer: We've had a fair amount of expansion into new markets, which we're quite pleased with, but growth simply hasn't occurred as quickly as we'd hoped. We need to hire people who know how to motivate *other* people and boost performance across the board.

You: I like the idea of being involved in changes that enhance the growth of a company and move it in a more positive direction. I've always worked well with people and seem to be able to mobilize others to get things done. Last year, I ran our college blood drive and got a record number of people to donate. I encouraged every college student to bring a friend to the drive, and everyone who came received a free ticket to a campus dance.

Interviewer: It sounds like you're good at getting your classmates motivated. But have you ever influenced someone who wasn't a peer?

You: One example comes to mind. My friend's father was running for mayor of our town. It was a close race, because the incumbent was well known. I volunteered to be part of the team that went door-to-door to invite people to a "Meet the Candidate" event. This was really about being a salesperson, and I had never done anything like it before. But my friend's father had really been a kind of mentor to me, and he always gave thoughtful advice—so I could persuade people by discussing his positive attributes honestly and sincerely. When I went to the event, I was pleased to see how many families came that I had personally talked to.

Interviewer: Just curious—did your friend's father win?

You: Unfortunately, no. But I think we all learned a lot from the experience.

Interviewer: Some people are reluctant to sell anything or approach strangers with their opinions. But business is a lot about selling—products and ideas. It sounds like you got yourself some good experience.

Questions to ask about the job

Questions about the job fall into two general categories:

- Technical (if the job requires specialized training or education)
- General

It would be impossible to list all the technical questions you might ask, if you are going into a specialized field. However, most of the questions you will want to ask are probably more general. Here are some questions you might ask about the job:

- What is the goal of this job?
- What are the most important responsibilities of the job?
- What technology will I be expected to know and use?
- On which tasks would I spend most of my time?
- What would a typical day (or week) look like for me?
- What are the most difficult aspects of the job?
- Will I have independent projects, or work as a team?
- Who will evaluate my performance? My boss? Others?
- What criteria will be used to evaluate my performance?
- What is the work schedule? At what hour will I be expected to begin work? When do most people leave work for the day?
- Is any special training, education, or background required?
- Will I receive training for the job?
- How often would I be evaluated for promotion?
- What is the next step up from this job?

Mobilizing your success stories

The beauty of asking questions and getting information is that it sometimes puts you in the position of helping—offering your skills, experiences, or special abilities to either solve a problem or simply "pitch in." If you listen carefully to the way your interviewer responds to your questions, you will get a strong impression of what the goals of a job are. The next step will be to use your success stories as a sales tool: Your objective is to convince your interviewer that you are the most qualified person for the job. Your strategy is to match your success stories, each of which contains a desirable success factor, with as many of the job's goals as possible. You might begin a dialogue this way:

You: "Will I always work on a team, or will I handle some independent projects?"

Interviewer: There will lots of opportunities for both. Luckily, the people in this company generally work well together: There's lots of teamwork between senior and junior personnel and between departments. And, of course, some jobs are team-driven. However, in our office, I will need you to do a lot of independent work. It's an important feature of the job. I won't be able to supervise your projects all the time because so much of my work involves meetings and travel, so I'm looking for a certain level of independence and autonomy.

You: I'm very glad to hear that you're so supportive of independent work, because solving problems and managing projects on my own is one of my strengths. It's always been important for me to plan, organize, and set priorities, so I have very good work habits. To fulfill the requirements of my molecular biochemistry and biophysics major, I worked on a long-term independent project my senior year. My work involved proving the effectiveness of a certain method of isolating proteins. Despite very little supervision, I fulfilled all of the project requirements and even came up with a couple of surprising conclusions. The work was very exciting and helped prepare me for a job as a research assistant in a pharmaceutical lab.

Interviewer: Deadlines are essential, of course, but you do want to know that the person you've entrusted with an independent job can actually do good work without your constant supervision. So, you don't think that will be a problem for you?

You: No, I don't think so. As long as I'm clear on objectives, goals, and deadlines I'm in good shape. One of the best aspects of a science background is that it teaches you how to ask good questions. This has really helped to direct my activities and point me in the right direction.

Is there any doubt in your mind that you're making a good match with the job and your prospective employer? Notice how he took *your* lead in his last response. *He* summarized the points you'd just made and *he* stated that you probably wouldn't have a problem achieving the goals of one of the most important aspects of the job.

It's clear that your story has done a good job of proving your claim to being a good independent worker. Some of the other success factors that were illustrated so effectively in this story include:

- Accomplishments/Getting Results
- Initiative
- Problem Solving
- Project Management
- Handling Pressure

Keep in mind that when you're telling one of your success stories in order to "sell" yourself, you're not bragging. That's not the point. You want to get a job because of your merits and, in order to do that, you must give the interviewer a good sense of your strengths. Telling your stories is all about facilitating the process of decision making. You simply want to make your appropriateness for a job as obvious as possible to your interviewer. And, of course, you need to know for yourself if a job is right for you. The most effective way to get that information is to keep the flow of conversation between you and your interviewer direct and clear.

Making opportunities

Don't forget to listen very carefully to your interviewer's responses: He may be telling you that he's interested in your accomplishments and wants to know more about them. It's always a bonus for you to provide more information because of the supporting evidence it adds to your claim of being the most qualified person for the job. Here's an example of how this might work.

Interviewer: What was the most important aspect of the summer job you just mentioned?

You: I had a lot of responsibilities, but the one that interested me the most was keeping the connection between editors and authors alive. The editors I worked with were so busy they didn't have time to maintain regular contact with authors. Consequently, some authors felt some resentment. They no longer felt committed to the publisher or responsible for delivering their manuscripts on time. I began to see that the publishing schedule was becoming compromised—we just weren't going to be able to publish some books on time. I had to do something. So I took the initiative, and it became my job to keep the line of communication open between authors and the publisher, even if there was no direct, daily contact with the editors.

Interviewer: That's interesting. Can you give me a few more details about what you did to keep the connection with the authors alive?

You: Well, my company had just undergone a merger so things were a little disorganized: the editors had extra work and the authors were concerned that their books would get lost in the shuffle. To make sure that the authors felt comfortable, and that our books were published on time, I made up a spreadsheet that tracked due dates for each stage of each project. Included in the spreadsheet were regularly scheduled follow-up phone calls. Each author received a copy of the schedule, so he knew how his book was progressing and when we would be in touch. I e-mailed the authors regularly, just to check in and make sure that there were no problems—and it was also a great way to remind them of deadlines. The authors were reassured about their importance to the company and were accountable for their deadlines. And the three senior editors I worked with were delighted that I took the initiative to keep the lines of communication open between "their" authors and the publisher, even if they didn't have the time to make direct, daily contact themselves. Suddenly everyone was on the same page, and materials started to flow in again, despite all the uncertainties of the merger. Sometimes people just need to be reassured that everything is all right, and that someone is looking after their interests. After all, the authors were our customers, and, in order to succeed, a company has to assure customers that they are receiving the best possible service.

Interviewer: I think you're right. One of the things we really need in this company is better customer service. The service we provide is generally quite good, but a portion—a certain population—of our consumer base has been out of sync with us for over a year. We don't want to lose these customers—or our market niche—but we're not quite sure how to reach them. We've tried a couple of things, but it's too soon to see results. We need people who communicate well and who are extremely responsive to our customer's needs. It sounds like your experience at that publishing house was similar. You took the initiative to keep the company's authors in line and the product in place. That interests me.

By now you've planted a seed in the interviewer's mind and it will continue to grow. In essence, you've made a sale. Your success story has hit a responsive chord with your interviewer and you can practically see his mind working: "This candidate is very strong. This young woman has all the right stuff to be groomed for a major, creative spot in customer service. Her experiences indicate that she'd be extremely effective at this sort of work. Her story is very convincing. We need to get those customers back. Can I afford to pass up this opportunity to hire someone who might help reverse a serious downtrend in the company's service record? We need people who can take initiative."

When you make an opportunity for yourself and do it honestly, you shouldn't worry about having used a little sales savvy to get there. An effective success story is simply a distillation of what is truest about you.

Before you leave the interview

You've hit that moment in your conversation where it's clear there's nothing more to be asked, answered, or discussed—at least for now—and it's time to go. Your interviewer has stood up. He's smiling. He's put his hand out, you've shaken it and smiled, and now you're both headed toward the door. How are you going to leave things so that you're still in the driver's seat? Quick, before your interviewer says something polite like, "Well it was a great pleasure to meet you. Have a good day" you need to re-open the door. You might say something along these lines: "Thank you so much for your time. I've enjoyed talking with you too, and I believe

I have something special to offer your company. Can you tell me when I might next hear from you, or if there is anything else I can tell you about myself?" Or, you might say, "It was a pleasure speaking with you. What's the next step in the hiring process?"

If more than one person is involved in the decision, you can leave with these parting words: "When might I hear the committee's decision about the job?" Contrary to what you might believe, there's nothing "pushy" about conveying urgency. If anything, it demonstrates that you're serious about getting the job. It also says that you take yourself seriously and value the contributions you'd like to make to the company. This is a positive, active, and memorable way to take your leave.

In Chapter 4, we discussed how to follow up after an interview. You may wish to go back and review the steps to take in order to keep you and your resume at the top of the interviewer's pile. Here's the quick version:

- Give yourself an evaluation. What went well? What would you do differently next time?
- Write a thank-you note to everyone you met with while the interview is still fresh in your mind.
- Mark your calendar for a follow-up phone call with the HR department or interviewer to see how the decision-making process is proceeding.
- Take your suit or interview "uniform" to the dry cleaner to get ready for your next appointment, and plan what to wear if you get called back for a second interview tomorrow.

The most important point to get across in any type of interview setting is the broader picture of who you are. Your potential employer wants to know what you have to offer her beyond what you have included in your resume. Each person who interviews you wants to know how you think, how you react, and how you use your judgment so that he or she can make a well-informed decision about whether or not you will be a valuable addition to the company. When you use specific examples from your past experience to illustrate your accomplishments, you are proving your claim that you do in fact have the skills she is looking for. However, you must not be so eager to tell your success stories that you never answer the actual questions you are asked. Make sure to focus on your listening skills; answer the questions you are asked and then move into your stories to present yourself in the best possible light. And don't forget to follow up! Be proactive and find out what the next step of the interview process will be. If you really want to move on to the next step, you must take the initiative; you don't want to leave your future in someone else's hands.

Pearl of Wisdom

DON'T UNDERSELL THE VALUE OF YOUR PREVIOUS EXPERIENCE.

"When I interviewed for a new corporate job, I made sure to call attention to my restaurant management experience. When you think about it, this experience really reveals to the interviewer that you can handle responsibility. Translated into the corporate world, this means I know how to supervise a staff, manage multiple tasks (ordering food, making sure it arrives, helping to plan menus, resolving any customer complaints, etc.), ensure that everything runs smoothly, and organize the big picture; all of these skills are integral to running a business."

—ANDY, SALES DIRECTOR

other types of interviews and how to handle them

Off-site, Group, Panel, Campus,
Case Study, Recruiter, and Internal Interviews

THE BEST WAY to prepare for any interview is to continue to hone the skills you've learned and developed, such as researching, listening well, preparing questions and answers, and editing and diversifying your success stories. You simply can't go wrong if you bring the same level of organization, alertness, and enthusiasm to every interview. At the same time, it helps immeasurably to know the nuts and bolts of each kind of interview, as we saw in Chapter 5.

Although it is true that most interviews share the same features, a few have pronounced differences. For example, a panel interview involves several interviewers—a difference that requires the interviewee to answer questions more concisely than he might in a standard interview, where there is more room to be expansive. Learning how to gauge your skills and responses to differences in interviewing techniques and styles requires flexibility and a willingness to improvise. But with a little preparation and practice you should be able to handle the dynamics of any interview setting.

The key is to be as proactive as possible: Become involved in the interview process rather than letting it roll over you. And rather than dwell on the constraints of a particular form of interview, look for opportunities to show your strengths and best qualifications for a job. If you don't lose focus of your objective and have the courage to direct—and even re-channel—the flow of questions and answers you are guaranteed to have a great interview. The first step is to know what will be expected of you in each interview scenario. This chapter begins with a familiar form—the traditional interview, which is discussed at length in Chapter 5. Here, it goes off-site. As you will see, your skills and modus operandi will have to adapt to a change of location, but the information and advice below should help smooth the way. Finally, be aware that thoughtful and prompt follow-up is required of every form of interview. Use the opportunity of writing a thank-you note or making a phone call to consolidate and preserve the good impression you've already made.

OFF-SITE INTERVIEWS

Off-site interviews are generally conducted over a meal—lunch or dinner—in a restaurant. There are a number of reasons why you might be asked to attend an off-site interview. Your interviewer may prefer to meet you without office distractions, or may work in a small office where the two of you could not have privacy. If your prospective job involves meeting with clients or being in the public eye, the off-site interview may be a test of your social graces.

Standard etiquette

No matter what the reason for your off-site interview, you should make sure that you're well-versed in the rules of etiquette. In order to prepare yourself for the meeting you should peruse the pages of a standard book of etiquette, such as *The Amy Vanderbilt Complete Book of Etiquette* (revised edition, 2000). This is not to assume that you have no manners, but rather to help you to be more comfortable with the situation. You will feel more confident knowing that you double-checked which bread plate belongs to you. Whether or not the job involves entertaining clients, your prospective supervisor will be looking for a certain level of poise in social settings.

The interview will likely be fluid and more conversational in tone. However, it is still in your best interests to consider it a test. Although you and the interviewer may discuss a recent film or a book you just read, remember that this is still an interview, not a meal with a friend.

On a purely pragmatic level, it makes sense not to order a dish that will be difficult to manage, such as lobster or spaghetti, unless, of course, you are extremely adept at handling both. But then there's the drinking dilemma.

Should I order a drink?

The best rule of thumb is: never drink at an interview. Even if your host is drinking, it is not a good idea to follow suit. Although you may think you handle alcohol well, it is very easy to lose your focus and self-control if you drink. And if you don't handle alcohol well, do not order it under any circumstances, even if your potential boss orders a glass (or bottle) of wine, a beer, or a cocktail.

Following up

Don't leave the interview, even if it is at a restaurant or in the company cafeteria, without finding out what the next step is. Who will be calling whom? And, of course, you need to send a thank-you note. Typically, a note is handwritten on stationery or printed out on the same paper with the same heading style as your resume and cover letter paper. Writing a note shows that you have taken the time—instead of quickly dashing off an e-mail—to express your thanks in a thoughtful and personal way. Remember to refer specifically to something you discussed over the meal that reinforces how well suited you are to the job. If you are not sure how to write a thank-you note, almost any book of etiquette will show you how, or refer to the sample in Appendix D.

Regarding thank-you notes: Mailing an actual note is the best option, but in today's business world, e-mail is often the norm, especially when hiring decisions are being made quickly. The key to any thank-you communication is to be courteous, concise, and timely.

GROUP INTERVIEWS

A group interview involves meeting with several different people over the course of a few hours or a day. If you are interviewing for a paralegal position at a large law firm, for instance, you might meet with a human resources administrator, a financial manager, several attorneys, and one or two paralegals, in addition to your prospective boss. The reasons for being interviewed by a group may vary, but in most cases you will have already taken these two steps before you are asked back to meet more people:

1. A screening interview with someone from the Human Resources department
2. An interview with your potential boss

The people you'll meet are either in your potential department or work with it, in one capacity or another. The most important thing to remember about this kind of interview is that while your potential boss's opinion of you counts the most, he or she would not have asked others to interview you if their vote didn't count also.

In the best-case scenario, the majority wins: if almost everyone—say five out of a group of six (including your potential boss)—agrees that you are the best candidate for the job, then you are hired. In the worst-case scenario, a consensus is called for, and you don't get hired unless everyone agrees that you should get the job.

Needless to say, it is important to do well in all of your interviews, whether it is one-on-one with someone in human resources or with a group of potential co-employees. Part of the test in being interviewed by many people is getting along with all of them. Very often the feeling is, "Oh well, I didn't have chemistry with the financial manager, but I did with the marketing person, so they'll cancel each other out." However, that might not be true. Try to build rapport with everyone. Listen for clues about what is most important to each person; once you know, you can expand your answers to include relevant details.

Sometimes the interviewing group is made up of your peers, which may make you feel more comfortable and will give you an opportunity to learn about company culture from your peer group. Be careful, though, about the questions you ask. Your potential boss will undoubtedly ask members of the group what you talked about, and it could seriously work against you if he or she discovers that you kept asking everyone what the promotional opportunities or vacation policies are, especially if you've already covered this ground with your potential boss. It'll look like you're "checking out" what he or she told you or that you're less focused on the job itself than on the job's benefits.

Group strategies

When you're talking to a lot of different people, you won't have as much time to get across as many stories as you did during the interview with your potential boss, so you'll have to be selective about the ones you use. For example, if you're chatting with a financial person, you'll have to work in a short story that demonstrates your numbers savvy; if you're talking to a marketing person, pick a story about when you've used creative ideas. So it's important to understand your audience: What is this person's function in the organization, and which of my stories would be the most compelling and relevant to their particular experience?

"After my first interview at an advertising company, I was called back for a group interview. I was a little nervous about having to sell myself to so many people in a single day—after all, one interview is exhausting, so I figured five or six would be grueling. But then a friend told me a little trick to make things go more smoothly. She said that one way to make the interviews easier was to incorporate what the one person had told you about the company into your interviews with others. It sounds simple, but it really works. My first interviewer told me a bit about a recent, untraditional ad campaign the company was involved in. So, when I met with the second interviewer, I mentioned the campaign and asked if the firm was planning to continue exploring innovative advertising methods. I was even able to tie our discussion in with a story about how I had used some unorthodox, but very successful, methods to boost the number of advertisers at my college yearbook. As I learned more information from different individuals, I incorporated it into my next interviews. I was more relaxed, and I came across as very knowledgeable and interested in the firm. And, best of all, I got the job."

—CRAIG, ADVERTISING

Following up

After a group interview, make sure you thank your potential boss for giving you the opportunity to meet with some of the people you might be working with. Don't leave without asking him or her what the next step is. If it's up to you to call someone in human resources or your potential supervisor by a certain date, make sure that you do. In the meantime, send individual thank-you notes to the people you met. Take the time to write a thank-you note to your interviewer. It is important to reinforce your interest or to express renewed enthusiasm for the job.

PANEL INTERVIEWS

During a panel interview, you will meet with several people at the same time. This type of interview will simulate a business meeting where you are the presenter. The members of the panel will be people with whom you would interact when on the job or a group of individuals designated because of their status, skills, and areas of expertise as an "Employment Committee." The panel might include your potential supervisor, his boss, someone from human resources, coworkers, plus one or more senior managers who might be tangentially involved with you and your work. The interview usually lasts for about an hour, although it could be longer.

Even if you are scheduled for a panel interview, you will still have a one-on-one interview with your potential supervisor, which should last at least an hour. The interviews don't necessarily occur on the same day. In any case, a panel interview typically follows a standard progression: Stage one is the interview with human resources; stage two is the interview with your potential supervisor. On-campus panels take place at a college or university; in these interviews, students will be asked to come into a room, one at a time, in order to be interviewed without the benefit of meeting with anyone from the company beforehand. In other words, this arrangement would take the place of a screening interview. If all goes well, the student is brought back to the employer's location for the second stage of the interview.

The Protocol

The person who moderates a panel interview is usually the most senior person in the room. The arrangement varies from company to company, although it should be fairly clear who the moderator is because she will be the person to set the stage for you. For example, the moderator might start out by introducing the members of the panel and then launch into the objective of the interview. Pay attention to both points and quickly jot down notes to help you remember the names of the panel members. The moderator will then tell you what the next steps will be. Usually it is a straightforward affair: Members of the panel ask questions and you answer them until the hour is up or the questions seem to come to a natural stopping point.

There is no limit to the number of people who might be on the panel: There may be as many as six or more or as few as two. As discussed above, the composition of a panel varies depending on the nature of the job, so don't be surprised if there is someone on the panel who might actually be your peer. If the company expects you to work in teams with people from various levels of the organization, it makes sense to meet them early on. The main advantage of the panel is that it saves time. Everybody hears your story firsthand, so it's a very efficient way of interviewing.

However, panel interviews can be very stressful. This is something that most candidates underestimate. It is challenging to build rapport with each panelist. Also, panel members don't always decide before the interview what types of questions will be asked and who will ask them. So, while you're answering one question, the panel members are busy thinking of the next one. This rapid-fire questioning technique can be both hectic and demanding, and it requires that you think on your feet.

Strategies for panel interviews

In your effort to create some sort of structure to reduce the stress of being asked so many questions by so many people at such a fast rate, the tendency is to focus on answering the questions of one person on the panel. This is a mistake. Instead, you should try to include all members of the panel in the discussion. Make eye contact with the person who has asked the question, but make sure you include others by making eye contact with them as well. (See Chapter 5 for more information about using—and reading other people's—body language in an interview.) If you can, tie comments made by one member of the panel into your answer of another member's question.

The second mistake you can make in a panel interview is to be reactive rather than proactive. On one hand, it is very important to pay attention to the questions and make sure you answer them. On the other hand, you want to maintain some control of the interview and tell some of your success stories. First focus on answering the questions that are being asked, and then switch your focus to using your success stories. Take a look at this sample interview to see how you might accomplish this:

Panel Member 1: Why did you choose to go to Humboldt College?

Tyler: I chose Humboldt for several reasons. I knew that I wanted to go into journalism, and Humboldt has an excellent writing program, as well as a well-respected college newspaper—

Panel Member 2: Yes. I see here that you were managing editor of the newspaper. So you decided to do that to gain experience in journalism?

Tyler: That was certainly part of it. But I also chose to work on the paper because of the leadership opportunities the job provided. As managing editor, I was responsible for supervising a staff of forty-five columnists and editors. I didn't just have my own deadlines—I had to keep track of and manage everyone's deadlines. I created a computer tracking system that sent automatic e-mails to columnists, reminding them that their column was due in one week, two days, and one day. The reminders worked wonders, and because columns were in on time, the editors and layout staff were able to produce the paper in a timely manner—instead of being forced to pull all-nighters. So, I decided to work on the paper to learn about journalism, but also to tackle a leadership role and to prove that I could implement creative ideas to make an organization run more smoothly.

Tyler could have gotten flustered when the second panel member interrupted him. Instead, he capitalized on the panel member's question, using it to tell a story that demonstrated his initiative and leadership and problem-solving abilities.

You may actually find it much easier than you expected to get out your success stories, because people will be asking you *a lot* more questions than they would in any other setting, including group interviews. However, don't get nervous if you can't get all ten stories out—five or six is plenty. So, before you start freewheeling and talking off the top off your head, remember your strategy:

- Don't wait to work in your success stories if you see possible segues. It is just as important to illustrate your good qualities by way of success stories in a group as it is during a one-on-one interview. Remember to answer each question directly, if necessary, and then launch a story.
- If the panel asks you questions for which you have no prepared story, you will have to think on your feet. Pause, collect your thoughts, and improvise. Keep these answers short, and save your time for the success stories that you've prepared.
- Try to give the panelists equal time. Providing thorough answers to each question ensures that you've given respectful, thoughtful answers to each member.

If you tell your stories in a compelling way, your audience will want to hear more. If you've ever made a speech, delivered a paper, or made a presentation in class, you know the drill: People ask questions afterward. If your topic has been particularly stimulating, they get excited and start asking questions simultaneously, without waiting for each other. In this situation you may feel relaxed because you know your subject and feel in control of it. You should feel the same way about a panel interview because the subject matter is *you*. Prepare to talk about yourself as you would any other subject of a speech or presentation. Before the interview, go over the ten stories that describe your best qualities over and over again. Think of ways to weave them into the kinds of questions that might be asked of you. Here are some sample questions that do not specifically ask for stories. Pay attention to the answers, noting the way the speaker used the questions to segue into his stories.

What are your greatest strengths?

I am levelheaded, efficient, and I'm very persistent. I think my greatest strength, however, is creative problem-solving. I'm good at looking at problems and thinking of ways to fix them. For instance, I spent one summer working at a doctor's office. The administrative assistants did all the billing by hand—it was an arduous process. I knew there had to be a better way, so I did some research on computerized billing programs. I found one company that would come to the office and spend half a day training the employees, without charging any more than the other services. I also volunteered to learn all the intricacies of the program myself, so that I could assist anyone who had trouble using the system. Within a couple of weeks, things were running smoothly—and all of the assistants had extra time to devote to other tasks.

How do you usually handle conflicts?

I try to keep cool when dealing with a difficult situation. I think it's important to solve problems by reasoning, rather than letting personal issues get in the way. I often had to deal with conflicts when I was editor of my high school yearbook. I had a very large staff, and there were often huge disagreements over what photos to print, how to lay out the pages, how to spend our budget, and so on. In addition, there were many clashing personalities—some of the staff members had trouble getting along with others. During one meeting, the arguing got so bad that we simply couldn't get anything done. Instead of losing my temper, I decided that we had to implement a better system of running meetings and making decisions: a set agenda. Everyone received a copy of the agenda, so there was no confusion about what would be discussed; I always factored in time for people to bring up other issues, but the agenda gave the meetings structure. We also voted on all decisions, and a decision could only pass if three-fourths of the staff agreed to it. Meetings ran much more smoothly after that, and there were fewer arguments.

There is a third mistake that panel interviewees sometimes make: They assume that they have to get everything "right," but have no idea what "right" means. Relax. This is not a true/false quiz. The panel will evaluate all of your answers, your communication style, your poise, and many other factors. There is no "right" answer that will get you the job. As with all types of interviews, prepare yourself by doing your homework on the company and get a good night's sleep.

REMEMBER TO . . .

- Bring pencil and paper. It's impressive if you can address the people on the panel by name, although you don't have to every time. Think of a way to remember people's names. In all the nervousness at the beginning of an interview it's all too easy to forget them.
- Before the interview, ask the person who is organizing the panel to tell you who will be on it, so that you'll have the names in front of you. In order to help you connect the names with faces, give each name a number. Then draw a little dais on a piece of

paper. As soon as a panel member identifies him or herself, insert the number on the dais where the person is sitting.

- Get a good night's sleep.
- Try to relax as much as you can.
- Breathe regularly; holding your breath will make you tense.
- Don't talk too fast: Slow down. You'll be able to speak more clearly and convincingly if you give yourself a little time to think.
- Stick to your objective.
- Don't leave without telling as many of your success stories as possible.
- Maintain steady eye contact, focusing on the person who asked the question, but including the others as well; don't let your eyes jump around too much.

Following up

If a panel interview is either on the same day or within a day or two of a one-on-one interview with your potential boss, write her a thank-you note, and be sure to write individual notes to everyone on the panel. It is also a courtesy to thank your potential employer for arranging the panel interview. Remember to point out anything that came up in the panel interview that was of special interest to you or which relates to your particular fitness for the job.

If you really want to move on to the next step, you must take the initiative; you don't want to leave your future in someone else's hands.

CAMPUS INTERVIEWS

Some campus interviews occur at career fairs, which gives them an entirely different feel than traditional interviews. For one thing, you have less time to present yourself in the best light. In fact, you don't usually have more than three minutes to get your sound bite out at an employer's booth or table. Some companies conduct mini-interviews in an auditorium or hall that is filled with hundreds of other students who are trying to get the same job. Under these circumstances, what you have to do is get your resume into the hands of the right person and make sure that he or she remembers you during the screening process.

Making an impression

If you have only three minutes in which to sell yourself—and that's exactly how long most campus interviews really last—it is extremely helpful to research the company first and rehearse what you want to say. (Please refer to Chapter 3 for more information on researching a company.) You will greatly boost your chances of being taken seriously if you can say that you are interested in the company for very specific reasons and that your background is a good fit for the job because of specific reasons. In any case, you won't have time for even one good success story, so you'll have no choice but to focus on facts. Be prepared to know what they are and make as compelling a case as you can for yourself. Don't be shy. Campus recruiters expect a hard sell because of time limitations and the sheer number of students who want to be interviewed. Once you get a date for a second interview, you can work on presenting yourself at length—and with a little more polish.

On-campus recruiting

Your college or university may also participate in on-campus recruiting. This means that you can set up interviews with certain firms through your college career center. The interviews will take place on campus.

The companies that participate in on-campus recruiting tend to be large firms that hire many new employees straight out of college.

The types of companies that recruit vary widely depending upon which college you attend. Be sure to speak with your college career center to see how on-campus recruiting works at your school. Some schools arrange a "resume drop," a day when students wishing to participate in on-campus interviews must file all resumes and cover letters with the college career center. Typically, students will have to prepare a separate resume/cover letter package for each firm to which they wish to apply. If your college has such a system, be prepared—resume drops may occur as early as December, although interviews may not be scheduled until February or March.

What to expect

On-campus interviews are screening interviews to decide which candidates will be invited back to the company for further interviews. A company interviewer may be your potential supervisor, human resources personnel, or an employee in a position similar to the one for which you are interviewing. Companies usually try to include one employee who graduates from your school. On-campus interviews are screening interviews; that is, the interviewers will meet with a number of students and then select a certain percentage of those students to move on to the next round of interviews. Although your interviewer will not be making hiring decisions, expect competition to be pretty stiff—on-campus interviewers will be seeing many qualified candidates.

CASE INTERVIEWS

If you are interviewing in certain fields, particularly consulting, financial services, and business development, you may be required to participate in one or more case interviews. In such an interview, you will be presented with a business problem, and asked how you would go about solving it. The goal of the interview is for the interviewer to gauge your analytical and problem-solving skills. The interview will *not* test your specific knowledge about an industry or business. Instead, applicants are typically presented with a generic scenario and may be given relevant information needed to solve the problem. As you work out the problem aloud, your interviewer will give you constant feedback and provide you with more information as you need it.

Cases can incorporate numbers and data to varying degrees. The interviewer may be interested in testing your ease with numbers and your quantitative abilities. If economic concepts are what the company is after (if, for instance, you are interviewing with a firm in financial services), they may instead deal with profitability or simple financial functions. In general, though, the most critical skills that case interviews screen for is the ability to think through problems in a logical, coherent manner with little preparation and limited information.

Case interview format

There are generally two types of cases that interviewers rely on.

Estimation cases or "mini cases" present the candidate with a numerical problem to solve with guidance from the interviewer. Although there may be a "right" answer, success does not depend on how close you come to this answer. Instead, the interviewer is more concerned with how you arrived at your answer and whether or not you can identify why you may be wrong. An example of the type of question you might hear at an estimation interview is, "How many pieces of luggage are unloaded at LaGuardia Airport each day?" To see how you might go about answering this question, and for more sample case interview questions, see Appendix G.

Business problem cases or "full case" interviews present the candidate with an open-ended business situation. Usually more complex and well developed than shorter estimation cases, these cases have no right answer and test your ability to think through issues to a conclusion that you can defend. An example of such a case would be: "Imagine that you are a consultant, hired by Carnegie Hall, a large concert hall in New York City. For the past several years, their profits have been declining, and they want you to figure out how to reverse this trend and restore profitability?" For a sample approach to this problem, as well as more information about tackling business problem cases, see Appendix G.

Helpful tips and tricks

Cases can seem daunting at first, but with a little practice, they can be a fun and interesting challenge, as well as the first step to a new job. Here are some tips and tricks from an experienced management consultant.

1. *Listen to your interviewer.* Generally, you will receive some guidance from the interviewer as you're answering the question. Pay close attention to the feedback that your interviewer gives when you ask questions, and be sure to incorporate his or her information into your analysis. There will be hints, explicit or implicit, in what the interviewer says. These can be very helpful.
2. *Get feedback after your interview.* No matter what the outcome of the interview, call your interviewer a few days later to get some feedback on how it went. If you're doing more than one case interview in your job search, the feedback will help you figure out what you're doing well and what you can improve.
3. *Keep a positive, inquisitive attitude.* A lot of the difficulty in cases is around getting over your fear of being wrong. Remember, there is no right answer! Instead of focusing on getting to the "right" solution, think of the case as an interesting challenge, and a chance to think creatively. You'll be surprised how much more open your thinking will be with the right attitude.

4. *Read the newspaper.* A good way to prepare for cases is to scan the business section of your local paper or the *Wall Street Journal.* Look for stories in which a company made a strategic decision, and think about what went into the decision. Make a practice case out of it for yourself.

5. *Go to a bookstore or library.* There are many books designed to help you deal with case study questions.

6. *Talk to an MBA or recent graduate who's been through the process.* See how they handled these types of questions. Get specific examples and methods.

INTERVIEWS WITH RECRUITERS

Recruitment firms are companies hired by other companies to fill vacant positions. Job hunters often use recruitment firms to find employment opportunities. Some recruitment firms are *not* interested in trying to place recent college graduates because their focus is on executive recruitment—head hunting for companies that want seasoned professionals. These are called "retained recruiters" or "retained search firms." They are hired on a long-term basis and paid by the employer, regardless of whether they find a candidate for every job or not.

Contingency firms

However, some recruiters *are* interested in recent graduates—recruiters in contingency firms, for example. These people are paid by the employer if the candidate they put forward is actually hired for the job. Recruiters in contingency firms find candidates from the college graduate pool in the following ways:

- From ads
- From their data base

- From resumes posted on the Internet
- Through their network

If you've responded to an ad by submitting a resume, you may get a call from a recruiter who is interested in interviewing you for a possible job. She may have found your resume posted on the Internet, or she may have found your name through her network. For example, suppose a recruiter who specializes in advertising jobs has a contact at the ABC Research Lab. You've recently applied to ABC and, although you have a very strong resume, you don't have the background in biochemistry that ABC is looking for. The recruiter calls her contact and says she is looking for a strong candidate for an advertising position: does the contact have any potential candidates? Your name and resume might be passed along to the recruiter.

The thing to remember about working with recruiting firms is that they are in the business of sales: They're not going to get paid unless they make one. Contingency recruiters don't have a lot of time to interview candidates in depth. Consequently, they're going to do a lot of screening as quickly as possible in order to get the right pool of candidates for a certain job. Therefore, you must do everything you can to make a lasting impression during a recruiting interview. For example, because recruiters are "in sales" and generally tend to be very high-energy people, it helps to emulate their level of energy and enthusiasm during an interview.

You may feel that the contingency firm is working for you—a feeling that the firm itself might promote, but remember that it is not doing anything for you *personally*. Remember that the firm is working first and foremost to get paid, and the only way that will happen is if it fills a job for an employer. The rub is that you aren't necessarily the only candidate the recruiting firm has in mind for a particular spot, no matter how special you're made to feel. Don't assume that just because you're listed with a recruiting firm you're taken care of. You need to use a variety of job search tactics to land a position.

....

MAKE THE MOST OF YOUR RECRUITING FIRM

In order to get the best possible service from your recruiting firm,
you need to do a few things.

1. Check in regularly. Recruiters constantly learn of new job
   openings—yours will be more likely to think of you for a new
   position if you're fresh in his or her mind.
2. Ask your recruiter how to "tweak" your resume to make it
   suitable for a wide variety of fields. Or, if your recruiter specializes in a certain area, ask how to better sell yourself to
   employers in that field.
3. Be flexible. If you place a lot of demands on your recruiter, he
   will have difficulty finding jobs for you.
4. Be honest. Be upfront with your recruiter about your experiences and skills. And always be sure to let him know if you
   are close to an offer with another employer.

....

If you are the proverbial round peg that fits the recruiting firm's
round hole, you'll be pretty high on its list. In other words, if you
have a background that matches what the recruiting firm's potential
client needs, it will be very motivated to work for you. After all, the
chances of getting a fee for placing you will be high. An example is
an accounting major who's looking for a job as a staff accountant
with a Big Five accounting firm. However, if you have an idiosyn-
cratic background, or if you're a liberal arts major, your position on
the recruiter's list will be lower.

Recruiting caveats

If you get a job offer through a recruiting firm, be careful: The
recruiter is going to put some pressure on you to take the job. His

objective, after all, is to make the placement. He has a vested interest in your taking the job—if you take it, he gets paid. Therefore, do not rely solely on the recruiter to be your mentor and co-decision maker.

As a person in business you will need recruiters in your life—when you're in your first job, for example, and looking for the next one. Definitely keep recruiters in your network. They are a valuable resource. Therefore, even if you don't take the job, make sure your recruiter knows that you value and have every intention of keeping him in your network.

A good way to keep in your recruiter's good graces is not to surprise him. For example, while your recruiter knows that you will be interviewing for positions without his help, he has no way of knowing when you are close to a job offer. Be sure to let your recruiter know when you're in the final round of interviewing at a company—that way, he won't be surprised if you turn down a job he found for you and accept a different job. You don't want to just disappear into thin air as a viable candidate. Your recruiter will feel that he is working for you, but you're not working with him. Therefore, use the same courtesy in this relationship as you do with your entire professional network.

Following up

Part of following up with a recruiting firm is keeping it in your network. Make contact with your recruiter periodically, even if it's just for a casual chat. Some businesses and industries are more volatile than others—so you may be looking for another job sooner than you think. Keep all of your options open. If the recruiting firm finds a job for you, send a thank-you note immediately.

INTERNAL INTERVIEWS

Internal interviews, those in which a current employee interviews for a job within his firm, will not be a concern for you until you've started to work for a company. Before you get hired, however, look into the company's policy about employees answering job postings, because it varies from place to place. Some companies actually have a bulletin board where job openings are posted. Under the best circumstances the company does not look for outside talent before it has investigated all the possibilities of hiring from within. Very often, insiders know about a job opening before it is even made public to other people in the company. Like so many other aspects of business life, "word gets around" before the official memos and postings do. If you work for a large organization, or one that has offices in various parts of the United States or overseas, it probably has a website for new job opportunities.

If you are interested in pursuing a job that has become available in your company, find out what the policy is before plunging ahead. For example, some companies insist that you go to your boss first, and tell him or her that you want to apply for another job, while others do not have such a requirement. The second factor to consider is your boss: Some bosses take pride in seeing the people they've hired move up, even if it means that an employee will be moving out of their department. These bosses are usually quite supportive. However, some bosses see "moving on" as a form of disloyalty. It is especially tricky to have this kind of boss if you interview for another job and don't get it. Your relationship will be somewhat strained afterward. Therefore it is essential to evaluate your boss, as well as the company policy, before interviewing for another job. You may want to have a confidential interview with human resources personnel to get advice on how to handle the situation.

The process

When it comes to internal interviews, employees in most companies follow a similar pattern:

- Stage one: an interview with the human resources department
- Stage two: an interview with the potential new supervisor

The most important criteria that human resource departments use to evaluate an employee for a new job include:

- Salary
- Skills
- Fit

Stage one interviews

The human resources department conducted your initial screening interview, of course, so they already know a great deal about you—how much money you make, for example, and how you were evaluated in previous performance reviews. However, you will have an opportunity to highlight recent projects, additional education, and outside activities that don't appear in your personnel file. The human resources person who interviews you will want to know all about what you've done in your current job and, more specifically, how it has prepared you for the prospective job. He or she will have little more than your original application to go on, so be sure to focus on what you've achieved since you joined the company:

- Update your resume: use it as a blueprint for your conversation with human resources
- Write a summary of what you've accomplished on your current job, or make a list of what you've accomplished
- List your achievements outside of work
- Point to successes on your last written performance review

If your last performance review noted an area that needs development, discuss the steps you've taken to improve your performance. If you've received any additional training or taken classes outside of work, such as computer programming, software design, business management, or even a foreign language course, list it after your job accomplishments. The same goes for other valuable experiences you've had outside of work, such as becoming the president of your alumni association or assuming a leadership position in your neighborhood or community. These accomplishments will say a great deal about who you are and where your values lie.

"Fit" is a little harder to gauge than salary or skills, because it has to do with your job performance and reputation in the company. For better or for worse, this is where your past will catch up with you. If you've had a complaint against you or been involved in some sort of conflict with a colleague, it will be factored, consciously or unconsciously, into the equation. Under these circumstances, the best thing to do is to bring up the subject and put it on the table. For example, Lucia and Julie were working together on a project and Lucia felt that Julie was doing none of the work. Naturally, there was a conflict, and Lucia and Julie found themselves in the human resources department in order to have the issue resolved. Six months later, Julie applied for a higher position in the company.

Once again, this is where skill at telling success stories comes in. In this case, Julie made it a point to show her maturity and ability to learn from her mistakes. She explained to a human resources administrator that after the conflict she took Lucia to lunch, and they discussed the situation and cleared the air. Now, they valued each other as colleagues. Julie's story was easy for human resources to substantiate. She received the promotion, not only because of her skills, but also because she was able to demonstrate her professionalism and maturity. So, if you've had conflicts at work, resolve them. You don't want past mistakes to preclude you from advancing in your career.

Stage two interviews

Interviewing with your prospective boss is different than any other interview situation described so far. First of all, you may have worked with her or someone on her staff as part of your current position. Perhaps she's had an opportunity to see you present your ideas at a meeting. Or maybe you've informally chatted during a company function. Whether or not you have interacted with her, you can be sure that your prospective boss has tried to do research about your performance record and your ability to work with others. This research will help her determine what questions to ask you and what issues she wants clarified before making a decision.

You can also do your own research through your informal network. Talk to people who can keep confidences and who know what skills and traits are valued by your prospective boss. You might also find out the goals and clients of the department to which you are applying and the reason that the position is open. This is exactly the kind of research you did when looking for your first job.

If you've worked effectively in the past with members of the department to which you are applying, you're in luck: The best reference you can get is a positive recommendation from your prospective boss or employees on her staff. Otherwise, think of people in the company with whom you have worked well and who regularly interact with your new department. You can cite examples of working with these people in your success stories. Keeping up your internal network will improve your chances of career advancement.

Although the interview itself will be conducted along the lines of a standard interview (please see Traditional Interviews, in Chapter 5, for guidelines) there are a few extra recommendations:

- Give your prospective boss a copy of your updated resume, even if the person in human resources says he already has a copy.
- Focus on the various skills you've learned from your previous job or from any training, classes, or courses you've taken outside the job since you first started working for the company.
- Use your success stories.

Because you've worked in the company, you should know the success factors that are highly regarded. An employee manual or your performance reviews may list skills that are particularly valued. If success factors aren't listed, ask your boss what it takes to achieve long-term success in your company. Once you know these factors, you can choose success stories that demonstrate the traits that are important to your organization. For example, suppose you work at an advertising agency and your prospective supervisor asks you what your greatest strength is. You might reply:

> *I think one of my greatest strengths is my ability to work well on teams. In the marketing department, most of our work was handled in teams. I always volunteered to take minutes of meetings and I used those minutes to draft agendas for future meetings. I also suggested that each team member take five or ten minutes at the beginning of every meeting to discuss what projects he was working on, where he needed help, and so on. Because we were organized and every member of the team was informed about what everyone else was doing, we were able to be efficient and avoid arguments. I learned a lot about building coalitions and handling disputes. I know that many of the projects in this department are also handled by teams, and I'm confident that I will work very well in that environment.*

At some point in the interview, you will be asked, "Why do you want to leave your current position?" It's important to give some thought to how you will answer that question, because your professionalism, maturity, and communication skills are being assessed.

In the best-case scenario, you've had ongoing conversations with your current boss about taking on more responsibility. He agrees that you're ready, but there's nothing available in your department. You've told him that you'd like to use internal posting when the right job comes up, and he agrees to be your coach to help you do well in the interview. This does happen and shows that the boss has the perspective to keep talent in the company. The one caveat is that he may ask you to time your departure to meet the business needs of the department.

There is, however, another scenario that's more challenging to handle. You've had conflicts with your boss over any number of issues—the work rules in the department, the assignments that you receive, how you've been evaluated, etc. So the reason that you want to leave has a lot to do with your boss. There is a strong likelihood that your prospective boss will be aware of this when it's time to get a reference from your current boss. So, the best thing to do is tell the truth, but communicate in the language of a professional businessperson. For example:

> *I respect my boss's authority and knowledge in his field. I've learned a lot about the insurance business from him. However, we don't always agree on how a project needs to be handled. I prefer to work more autonomously. He prefers to be very involved in projects. We've talked about this, and I don't feel I can do my best work unless I can make more independent decisions about projects that I'm responsible for.*

There is no benefit to talking negatively about a boss or co-worker. If you need to let off steam, you can do so with your friends and family. But in a business setting, there's an expected protocol. Even if you're justified in your complaints, your boss is being paid to direct the staff and make tough calls. You are being paid to implement his decisions in proactive, creative ways. If you demonstrate that you understand the company hierarchy and can maintain your professionalism even when your opinion differs from that of your boss, you will be more likely to advance in your company.

Finally, if you *do* get the job, make sure your new boss understands how important it is for you to be the first one to give the news to your current boss.

More diplomacy

Discuss with human resources personnel how important it is for you to be the one to tell your current boss about the new job— assuming, of course, that she doesn't already know that you've applied for another job within the company. It is simply a matter of courtesy to tell your boss that you are making a move before she hears it from somebody else. Don't put your boss in the embarrassing position of being caught off guard. As a businessperson, you do not want to burn any bridges behind you. In some industries, such as the fashion world, you run into many of the same people again and again as you move from one design house or retailer to another. And it is always good to know that you are well-regarded by them, especially if they have any say in whether or not you should be considered for a job in *their* company.

Make sure to give 100 percent during your last weeks in your current job. Finish all your projects carefully. If you will be handing off projects to another individual, be sure to leave detailed notes and try to work with your replacement before you leave. Also, remind your boss that you will be available to give help or information to the person taking over your duties. Leave your new phone number and e-mail address so that you can be easily reached.

If you don't get the job

If you are not accepted for the job, there may be two reasons for it:

1. Another candidate was better qualified or a better skills match to the open position.
2. There was something about your reputation that got in the way.

It may be difficult to assess accurately why you didn't get the job. Perhaps you lack certain technical or interpersonal skills. You may be unaware of these shortcomings, or you may have neglected to improve in weak areas noted on your performance reviews.

All too often, disappointed candidates don't take the time to find out why they aren't being considered for certain jobs. Instead, they may begin to feel hostile toward the company and their work suffers. To prevent yourself from getting stuck in an unsatisfying job or at a certain level, take steps to find out why you're not getting ahead.

- *Look into your company's policy.* Who should give feedback to candidates when they don't get the jobs they apply for? The person could be someone in human resources, or it might even be your own boss.
- *Tell the person you're disappointed* about not getting the job, but would like to learn from the experience. Ask for concrete information. Some of the questions you might ask are:

What did I do effectively in the interview?

What did I do less effectively in the interview?

What skills should I acquire, or which talents do I need to demonstrate, in order to be considered for a similar position within the company?

Is there something that I'm doing (or not doing) in my current job that is taking me out of the running for other positions in the company?

Some companies do not tell people why they don't get jobs, and expect their bosses to do all the explaining. But no matter what your company's policy is, it is a good idea to keep the channels of communication open between you and your supervisor.

To summarize, although the interview format may be different, the same basic idea holds true for any interview. Be prepared! If you know that you are going to have a very short time in which to sell yourself, have specific reasons ready as to why you are a good fit and why your background is suitable for the job. Use your success stories, be sure to answer the questions you are being asked, and link your success stories to the question. For case studies, you can prepare by practicing and being up-to-date on your current events. Although you don't know exactly what kinds of problems you will be required to work through, if you have done several practice problems, you will be more used to using your reasoning and problem-solving skills. What the interviewer really wants to know is how well you think and solve problems on your feet. When you interview with recruiters or for a different position within your current company, it is important to remember the networking skills you learned in Chapter 1. Make sure to both stay in touch and extend your network regularly; these steps will ensure that you have people working for you and people who are willing to help you at all times. And finally, no matter what type of interview you are participating in, don't forget to follow up. Thank the people who have taken time out of their busy days to speak with you. When you follow up you are proving that you have good interpersonal skills and are proactive; you are demonstrating professional qualities that everyone appreciates.

Pearl of Wisdom

DON'T TAKE PERSONAL CALLS OR BEEPER MESSAGES DURING AN INTERVIEW.

"I interviewed a woman for an entry level position at an advertising agency. I was in the middle of describing our company and what her position would entail, when her cellular phone rang. I was a bit annoyed that she hadn't turned her phone off, but even more perturbed when she asked me to 'Hold on a sec,' and proceeded to take the call instead of turn off the phone. At first I assumed that there must be some sort of emergency, but instead, I listened—shocked—as she made evening plans with her significant other. It was clear to me that she would not be right for the position, so I stepped up the pace of the interview in order to get her finished and out the door— and to make room in my schedule to accommodate the next candidate."

—SAMANTHA, PUBLIC RELATIONS DIRECTOR

C H A P T E R 7

troubleshooting

Tricky Questions; the Top 25 Interview Mistakes; the 50 Most Common Questions Asked; and How to Get Another Interview After You've Been Declined

NOT EVERY INTERVIEW is ideal: There are times when you get thrown off by a question or panic because you haven't been able to get across what you wanted to say. You might feel the need to correct something you've said or even change the course of an interview, but you don't know how. An interviewer may ask a question about your private life, your previous job, or your family background that you are not prepared for. Any of these situations can result in a disappointing interview.

Fortunately, there *are* ways to salvage interviews that go off course. The best strategy for steering the conversation away from dull, dead-end, or uncomfortable topics is to learn as much as you can about the job and the company *ahead of time* and prepare success stories and specific questions for your interviewer. If you've read about recent events or trends that might impact the company, or if it has developed a new product or service that might influence the job, talk about it. Ask questions. Try to keep sending the message that you showed up for the interview because you are interested in the job. Remember that an interview is a two-way process: If you give the interviewer the impression that you are bored or ill-prepared, you will not get the job. On the other hand, if you are interested and engaged, your interviewer will likely match your enthusiasm. So, if you feel that things are not going your way, take responsibility for the outcome. If you're interested in the job, you want to leave feeling that you did everything you could to put your interviewer at ease and convince him that you are the best-qualified person for the position.

This chapter arms you with information and strategies to help you anticipate tough questions, formulate responses, and get an interview back on course. With preparation, you should be able to go into any interview feeling confident and without fear of surprise or embarrassment. Preparation is the key: by researching and rehearsing what is likely to be asked, you are free to answer unanticipated questions with less stress and more confidence.

GETTING UNSTUCK: CHANGING THE COURSE OF AN INTERVIEW

You've showed up for your interview feeling alert and reasonably comfortable. The conversation was going well, but now the atmosphere has changed and your confidence is slipping. This can happen for a number of reasons, some of which were discussed in the introduction to this chapter, but in most cases an interview goes off course because:

- You have trouble answering a question
- Your interviewer is giving you a lot of information but not asking questions, and you're not sure how to convey your qualifications

- You wish you had answered a question differently
- You feel rushed by the interviewer
- You feel that the tone of the interview has changed

Not knowing the answer

Remember that most questions interviewers ask have no right or wrong answer. A good interviewer asks lots of open-ended questions that leave plenty of room for a variety of responses. But if you find that the only answer you can give to a question is "I don't know," relax. It's a temporary setback. You can always ask for clarification from the interviewer by saying, "I'm not sure that I understand the question. Would you mind restating it?" or you can ask that you come back to the question at the end of the interview.

If you have no information to add to an "I don't know" answer, you can always try adding a question of your own. For example: The interviewer has just asked you whether you know anything about the cosmetics division of the company. You might respond: "No, I don't. What part does it play in the major scheme of things here?" This response tells your interviewer that although you don't have the specific information she wants, you are nonetheless curious about the big picture. Your interest in learning more about the company's operations will not be lost on your interviewer.

It's one thing to feel dejected by an "I don't know" answer, but it's another to *look* it. If you hang your head, shuffle your feet, look terrified, or freeze up to the degree that you can't hear, let alone respond to, the next question, you will compromise your professionalism. So, even if you don't know the answer to a question and can't add either information or another question to it, don't let yourself get stuck. Stay poised and alert and wait for the next question.

It is important to remember that your interviewer is not trying to trap you or make you look uninformed. You can be sure that you and the interviewer share the same objective—to exchange information effectively, pleasantly, and in a timely fashion. Both of you have a vested interest in keeping the flow of conversation easy and open.

• •

Sometimes, your conversation with an interviewer may drift or come to a complete stop. To re-focus the interview, *ask questions* or *use your resume* as a guide to highlight your strongest qualifications and assets.

• •

Creating opportunities to present your credentials

Sometimes an interviewer focuses on talking about the company or the position without giving you many opportunities to talk about yourself. In these cases, the best thing to do is to turn the interviewer's approach into an advantage. If the interviewer seems most comfortable talking about the company, start asking questions about it. For example, if the company has changed direction in the last year, ask him what led to the change of direction. At some point you will exhaust the subject. But, by then, your summaries of information and the questions you've asked will have demonstrated not only that you've been listening, but that you've taken the time and initiative to research the company.

In addition, there is an acceptable way to interrupt. Everyone pauses, no matter how briefly, at the end of a sentence. When you hear that pause, make a statement about yourself that relates to what the interviewer just said. Look at the following example:

Interviewer: The company has grown so much in the last several years. We spend a lot of time communicating to our employees about our new business developments and new products.

You: I have some experience in that area. Last summer, I worked as a market researcher in a company that was promoting a new paint product. One of my tasks was to figure out how to get product information to the sales force on a timely basis. I conducted interviews with the sales reps and they told me they wanted an electronic newsletter, which I initiated. It was quite popular and eventually became an internal newsletter as well.

At this point, the interview can go in one of two directions:

- The interviewer is ready to hear about you
- The interviewer thinks the interview is over

If the interviewer is ready to hear about you, highlight your accomplishments by making a connection between yourself and what you've learned about the company. For example, if the company has taken a bold initiative to capture a new market this year, tie it into a story about risk-taking. Perhaps you can tell the story of how you devised an unusual promotion that doubled the number of subscriptions to your college literary magazine. Or perhaps you have another story to tell that emphasizes a tough decision you had to make, or a strategy that paid off. The point is to link your own risk-taking experiences with the needs of the company. Think back to some of the other points your interviewer made about the company and try to match your success stories to some of them.

On the other hand, if the interviewer gives you the message that the interview is winding down, don't leave before getting in at least one or two of your success stories. You might say, "Before I leave, I'd like to tell you a couple things about myself that relate to what we were talking about." Then launch into a success story. For example, perhaps your interviewer has just mentioned that the company is expanding its services to include foreign markets, such as Ecuador, Argentina, and Costa Rica. This is the perfect time to mention that you are bilingual. Maybe you majored in Spanish. Perhaps you even spent a semester in South America on a work-study program, and can describe some of your experiences in the South American business world. Choose stories that show your interviewer you understand the challenges of doing business with another culture and that you have the skills to meet those challenges.

We all learn by making mistakes. If possible, don't schedule your first interview with the job you want most. As you get more interview practice, you will feel more confident, know what kinds of questions to expect, and learn how best to present yourself. Practice your skills in informational networking interviews or in role-plays with a friend or mentor in the business world.

Saying what you want to say

Your interview is going well, when your interviewer asks, "What accomplishment are you most proud of?" You've prepared an answer to this question, but you have a sudden attack of nerves and draw a complete blank. You rack your brain and finally come up with a story, although you know it doesn't really show off your strengths. As soon as your interviewer asks the next question, you remember the story you had prepared. What do you do now?

If you've accidentally misspoken, continue with the interview and try not to let the statement throw you off track. Talk about your skills and accomplishments and ask questions, but wait to the end of the interview to correct a misstatement. After you've thanked your interviewer, tell her that you've been thinking about the way you answered one of the questions, and that you would like to expand on it quickly before you leave. If you don't realize that you misspoke until after the interview, you can always include the corrected answer in a thank-you note.

Feeling rushed

Occasionally, you may feel rushed by your interviewer. Perhaps something has come up—a deadline or a meeting—and your interviewer's body language and verbal cues are telling you: "I don't have much time." Or maybe your meeting has been delayed for some reason—perhaps the interviewer is still speaking with another candidate—and there isn't much time for your interview.

If you've scheduled back-to-back appointments or if your lunch hour at your current job is coming to a close (which means that you won't have enough time for this interview), simply say that you need to reschedule. What you do not want to communicate is disappointment, frustration, or, especially, anger. Instead, reiterate your interest in the company and in the position. Be understanding. Reassure your interviewer with a comment, such as "Unfortunately, I have another appointment in 30 minutes. It will be no trouble at all to reschedule the interview. I understand that appointments are sometimes delayed by other meetings or emergencies." Showing that you can be flexible in this situation will work to your advantage.

Salvaging a rushed interview takes a little more work—and confidence. Suppose your interviewer says, "Usually I take an hour for these interviews, but I only have twenty minutes." Take control of the process by asking, "What elements of my background would you most like me to talk about in the time we have?" If the interviewer begins talking, track where he or she is going. For example, the interviewer might want to discuss employment history, or your college major. After you've given a concise response, it would be perfectly appropriate for you to mention that there are only a few minutes left. At this point you could ask, "What are the most important things for me to tell you about myself in the time we have left?" If you know yourself and your success stories well, you will have no trouble finding one or two to illustrate those "important things."

Dealing with a change in the tone of the interview

Say the interview has been going well, but now your interviewer has been called out of the room. When she comes back, she has a different demeanor and the mood in the room has definitely changed.

Obviously something has happened. Once again, try to be flexible. Perhaps you could say, "If we're short on time, would it be helpful for me to tell you anything else about myself in particular?" In other words, take a proactive stance. Try to save the interview, but be diplomatic, especially if your interviewer is still visibly upset. Don't say, "What happened to you?" Communicate that you are aware that something has changed and offer to make things easier.

If the conversation has petered out or become too uncomfortable to move forward, suggest that you meet again at another time. You could broach the subject in this way: "If you would prefer to meet at another time, I would be more than happy to return when it is convenient for you."

Surprise questions

What if you're in the middle of an interview when you discover that you'd be working the third shift if you got the job? The challenge here is not to spill your coffee or burst out with "Really? Nobody told me!" Instead, try to be as calm as possible and say something that won't take you out of the running, such as: "I wasn't aware of that. Can you tell me more?" "How often and for how long would I work a late shift?" "Is that the permanent schedule, or would it apply only to the first ninety days?" In other words, keep the lines of communication open before you decide the job isn't for you.

Illegal questions

A number of state and federal laws make it illegal for interviewers to ask questions about your marital status, sexual orientation, age, nationality or ethnicity, or religion. On rare occasions, such questions may come up (usually because the interviewer is not aware that the question he asked is illegal). Think about how you will handle such a question if it comes up. You might ask how the information relates to the job, tactfully change the subject, or even answer the question if you feel comfortable doing so. For more information on illegal interview questions, visit the website of the federal Equal Employment Opportunity Commission (EEOC), at *www.eeoc.gov*. Many of the websites listed in Appendix B also provide information on illegal interview questions.

Questions about work schedule limitations

All employers need to know if the potential candidate can work the scheduled hours for the open position. You may get the question, "Does anything prevent you from working from 8 A.M. to 6 P.M. Monday through Friday?" While this question is perfectly legal, it can cause a candidate to disclose unnecessarily personal information about marital status, religious practices, or child or elder care. You must answer this question honestly.

If your religious observances prevent you from working certain hours, you need to tell the interviewer when you're asked that question. However, you should also add that in the past your religious practices have not interfered with you completing your class work or work with former employers. Be prepared to back up that claim with a list of references that will support your statement.

Familiarize yourself with the list that follows so that you know which actions are inappropriate, what comments to avoid, and what not to forget. You'll be glad you did—it could mean getting the job over another, less-informed candidate.

TOP 25 INTERVIEW MISTAKES

Familiarize yourself with the list that follows so that you know which actions are inappropriate, what comments to avoid, and what not to forget. You'll be glad you did—it could mean the difference between getting hired and getting passed over.

1. **Showing up late.** Be sure to allow yourself ample time to get to your interview. Be sure to factor in unexpected cir-

cumstances, such as train delays or heavy traffic. If you know you're going to be late, get to a phone at all costs so you can let your interviewer know.

2. **Being unprepared to describe your experiences.** An interview is a test—and you should never walk into a test unprepared. Take some time to prepare your success stories, and think about how you would handle the questions your interviewer might ask. Practice describing your experiences out loud or conduct practice interviews with friends.

3. **Answering questions with only a "yes" or "no."** Your interviewer needs to get to know you, and he will be unable to do that if you don't volunteer information about yourself. Be sure to support your answers with stories and examples.

4. **Fidgeting.** If you are tapping your foot, playing with a bracelet on your wrist, or constantly shifting in your seat, you won't look professional. And if you don't look professional, you won't get hired.

5. **Speaking too quickly.** You may want to get in a lot of information, but you don't want to speak so fast that your interviewer can't understand you. Take a deep breath before you begin answering questions and *slow down.* Conduct a practice interview with a friend to make sure that your speaking voice is steady and even.

6. **Avoiding eye contact.** If you avoid making eye contact, you will be unable to establish a personal connection with your interviewer. You should be attentive and engaged in what your interviewer is saying.

7. **Not researching the company.** Q: "What do you know about our firm?" A: "Uh . . . not much." Answers like this will not get you hired. Similarly, when your interviewer asks if you have any questions, you don't want to answer with, "Yeah. What exactly does this company do?"

8. **Lying.** Don't lie about or "embellish" your job experiences or academic record. Your interviewer is going to check these things out. If an interviewer catches you lying, you

won't be hired. If your employer finds out about your misrepresentation after you've been hired, you will be fired.

9. **Not answering the question asked.** You want to use your success stories in the interview, but you should be careful to always answer the question being asked. Don't be so intent on launching into a story that you avoid the question altogether—your interviewer will notice.

10. **Revealing too much.** Your interviewer is neither your best friend nor your therapist. She wants to learn about the skills and qualities you will bring to a job. She does not want to hear about your personal life or problems.

11. **Not "selling" yourself when you answer questions.** You should answer questions in a way that brings out the qualities that will serve you on the job. If you are asked how your best friend would describe you, don't say, "She thinks I'm a fun person and that I have great fashion sense." Instead, say something like, "I think my best friend would describe me as loyal and dependable. People always know that they can count on me."

12. **Speaking poorly of or belittling past job experiences.** Disparaging other employers or jobs will make you sound unprofessional, negative, and hostile. And it will make the interviewer wonder what you would say about *her* company to others. Try to focus on what you learned from other jobs.

13. **Dressing too casually.** Your interviewer wants to hire a responsible professional. Make sure you look like one.

14. **Not asking any questions about the company.** By asking some good questions, you will prove that you are very interested in the job—and that you were motivated enough to research the position and the company.

15. **Forgetting to send a thank-you note.** Demonstrate your professionalism and courtesy by sending a note. You will also be more likely to stand out in her mind if she has a reminder of the interview.

16. **Not thanking the interviewer at the end of the interview.** In the business world, a little courtesy goes a long way.

Your interviewer will appreciate and notice your good manners.

17. **Forgetting to bring a few extra resumes to the interview.** You may be asked for another copy of your resume, and you may have to submit an extra copy with any forms you have to fill out. Make sure that you're prepared.

18. **Neglecting to prepare a list of references.** Type up your references (with contact information) for your interviewer. He will *not* be interested in taking down all the names and numbers by hand, and it will inconvenience him if you have to send the information at a later date.

19. **Forgetting the interviewer's name.** You should always bring a note pad (preferably in a professional leather portfolio) to an interview. Write down the interviewer's name if you think you won't be able to remember it. Thank the interviewer by name at the end of the interview.

20. **Going to an interview on an empty stomach.** Remember when you took your SATs? You were probably warned not to take the test without eating, even if you usually skipped breakfast. The same goes for interviews. You will feel more alert if you've had a nutritious meal, and you won't get hungry if the interview ends up lasting much longer than you had anticipated. And, of course, you won't have to worry about your stomach rumbling in the middle of a question.

21. **Using filler words and slang.** Nothing makes you sound more unprofessional than peppering your speech with "like" and "y'know." Likewise, nothing will alienate your interviewer more than dropping slang into your responses. If you can't speak like a professional, your interviewer will question whether she can trust you to interact with clients or supervisors.

22. **Chewing gum, eating, or smoking.** These are obvious no-nos.

23. **Answering your cellular phone or pager.** Turn off your cell phone or beeper before you get to the interview. Better yet, leave them at home.

24. **Interrupting the interviewer or talking excessively.** Don't ramble or go off on tangents. You want to tell your stories and give the interviewer a good sense of your accomplishments, but make sure you don't cut the interviewer off or preclude her from asking questions. She has limited time to speak with you.

25. **Freezing up.** Relax! It's only an interview. If you're well prepared, you should feel confident and stress-free. Smile and be yourself. Your interviewer wants to hire a person, not a robot.

Experiencing the occasional tricky question or unexpected situation is inevitable. But if you think about how to approach—if not resolve—some of these situations beforehand, your chances of doing well and perhaps even acing an interview will be that much better. The secret is to stay relaxed and not to let temporary setbacks erode your confidence. Most potential problems are easily avoided if you maintain a poised and professional state of mind. You can even approach an embarrassing or difficult situation so that it works *for* you instead of *against* you. In the working world, tricky or delicate situations arise constantly; therefore, you might want to think of your interview as a test of how well prepared you are to handle them. By rising to each new challenge, whether it's thinking your way around a difficult question or putting a positive spin on it, you demonstrate your ability to adapt and be flexible—two skills that are well worth developing. Finally, taking a proactive stance to steer an interview away from inappropriate queries shows that you know how to take initiative and at the same time conveys persistence and endurance, qualities that will serve you well in the working world.

TOUGH QUESTIONS

Although many interview questions are straightforward and easy to answer, you will also face a number of tough questions. Tough questions are questions that require thoughtful, thorough answers;

they are questions that you don't necessarily expect or are difficult to prepare for. They probe more deeply into your claims than other questions. The purpose of these questions is to make sure you're answering consistently, to uncover additional information about your skills and accomplishments, and to gauge how well you think on your feet. It's important to know how to answer them well, because you will be asked these kinds of questions many times over the course of your professional life.

This chapter also includes a list of standard questions that are typically asked in interviews, along with a discussion of how to go about getting a second interview if you don't get the job. The emphasis here, however, is on succeeding—and if you are alert, well prepared, and primed to think on your feet, you will accomplish nothing less.

Handling tough questions

You will face a number of difficult questions during your job search. Below, you'll find some of the most common interview questions, as well strategies for answering them.

How would we benefit by hiring you?

Every employer wants to know what you can offer. What will some of *your* contributions be? Just because you're a recent college graduate doesn't mean that you don't have enough experience or skills to be valued as an employee. In fact, many of the skills you learned in school are very valuable in the workplace. For example, you probably worked on countless group projects; therefore, you know how to work effectively on a team. And if you participated in extracurricular activities you undoubtedly had to manage your time wisely between your family, friends, schoolwork, and other outside activities.

Depending on where the question about "what you can contribute" comes up in the interview, you can decide how many of your success stories you want to use. While you're scanning your memory for an answer, you can say, "Well, there are three things I believe I can contribute . . . " Why three? Because it genuinely helps to *think of a number*—especially when you're stumped on a question.

Pick a number, any number

Selecting a number—usually two or three—is a cue that focuses your mind, keeps you from freezing up during an interview, and organizes your thoughts. By the time you've selected a number and begun your answer, you should have a clear mental image of your list of success stories: Now, quickly select the two or three that best display your skills and talents. Don't repeat a success story that you have used before. If you've already told a story about your leadership skills on the job, but you want to highlight your abilities as a leader, choose a new story that shows you in another leadership role. Perhaps you were the captain of a sports team or ran a college club. Ideally, each of your success stories will illustrate a variety of skills; so, if you've already used your prima-ry "leadership" stories, you should have other examples that demonstrate leadership abilities.

What are you looking for in a job?

This can be a tough question, depending on when it is asked. If the question comes after you've been told about the job, and you know what the challenges are, you are ahead of the game. However, if you are asked the question *before* you've learned anything specific about the job, your response will have to be a little more general.

Sometimes a prospective employer will ask you about the kind of job you want, or the challenges that interest you, as a screening question at the beginning of an interview. The point is to see if your expectations match what the job has to offer. If you've been given details about the job, you can match them with the high points of your resume and some of your success stories; but if you don't real-ly know what the job is all about, you can't effectively link it to specific stories or skills. For example, if you are highly extroverted and social, you might be tempted to say that you're looking for a very people-oriented job. Having said that, you may learn that the job actually involves very little daily contact with other people.

If you find yourself in this situation, don't assume that the interview is over. Keep answering every question to the best of your ability. You may still be offered the job, in which case you'll need to find out more about the responsibilities and weigh the pros and cons of the position. Or, you may find out that there is another open position in the firm that you weren't aware of.

....

If you don't have a strong sense of what the challenges or requirements of a job are, but would like to buy time to learn more, keep your answers to questions about what you're looking for as open-ended as possible. Go back to the 10–point chart you made when reading Chapter 3, and choose some of the more general criteria for your ideal job. Almost any prospective employer will be happy to hear that you want to take on more responsibility, learn new skills, or gain a thorough knowledge of a particular field or industry.

....

Why are you the best person for the job?

If your interviewer asks why *you* are the best person for the job, it's important to link your reasons to information about the position and company. It may be that your technical skills, industry experience, and leadership abilities make you an ideal candidate for the job. Or perhaps you have the creativity, diligence, and interpersonal skills necessary to succeed at a particular company. The best answers to this question will contain at least three points that highlight your skills and career objectives.

What is the hardest thing you ever had to do?

Telling a success story about one of the most difficult things you've ever had to do—outside of the usual academic challenges of being a student—should focus on an action, something you had to *do* to overcome an obstacle or solve a problem. A success story that has anything to do with being an outsider or being thrown into a new or difficult situation where you had to sink or swim would be perfect for this question. Did you ever have to make the transition from living in a small town to living in a big city? What about being in a foreign country as an exchange student, and having to deal with another culture or language? Your first day as a summer intern in a law firm might have been a huge challenge, or maybe as a nurse's aid in between your sophomore and junior year you had to rise to the challenge of working in the emergency room and overcoming your fears.

Your story can be personal, but, once again, focus on the facts and the actions. For example, maybe you helped your family respond to a financial crisis by taking on an after-school job. One of the hardest things you may ever have had to do is achieve a certain level of excellence in order for your sports team to compete in a national or international contest. Describe what you did to overcome the problem. Any example or story you can tell that illustrates your determination, resilience, and perseverance will speak to this question.

What are your strengths?

It should come as a relief to answer this question. After giving so much consideration to your accomplishments and the things you're most proud of, you should have no trouble talking about the personal qualities you admire most about yourself. One approach is to focus on work strengths, such as organizational skills, ability to work in teams, or problem solving. Or, you might talk about traits such tenacity, maturity, or patience. If you're particularly proud of your ability to communicate well or think creatively, weave these characteristics into the stories you tell about yourself. Enjoy answering this question. You should have plenty of good stories to draw on, especially since you have devoted so much time to thinking of your own success stories. In order to prepare for this question, you might want to think about how your close friends or family members might describe you; you could even ask them for some suggestions.

What are your weaknesses?

The biggest mistake you can make in answering this question is saying, "I don't think I have any weaknesses that will affect my job performance." We all have shortcomings and you will not be penalized for revealing one or two of yours. If you have given this question some thought ahead of time, you should have no trouble answering.

The old advice was to choose a "bad" quality that is actually quite "good" in the context of a job. For instance, you may decide to say: "I tend to work very hard until the job gets done, and sometimes I shortchange my relaxation time." Although this approach can sometimes be successful, be very careful if you try to use it. Interviewers are on to this trick and will notice if you're not sincere or avoid revealing any flaws. Also, many people try to use this technique, and answers sound repetitive and disingenuous. Consider the following story:

> I was interviewing for a job in broadcasting. My interviewer had trouble framing one of her questions and finally asked, a little hesitantly, 'What do you think you most need help with at work?' I wasn't sure what she wanted, and I asked her to clarify the question. She said, 'I'm really trying to ask you what your weaknesses are. But I don't want to hear another candidate say, "I'm too much of a perfectionist" or "I'm such a hard worker that I don't give myself enough time to relax.' " I was very honest about admitting

my faults in some areas, and I made sure to demonstrate what I was doing to improve my shortcomings. I could tell that she appreciated my sincerity. And best of all, I got the job.

—Jeanne, Production Assistant

Don't be afraid to be honest. A good response to this question would be, "I think one of my weaknesses is that I'm not very outgoing when I first meet people or get thrown into a new situation. I like to take some time to step back and assess a situation before jumping in, and people sometimes mistakenly think I'm very shy or aloof. I've worked very hard on being more outgoing, though. Now, in any social situation, I try to talk to at least one unfamiliar person right away."

Where would you like to be five years from now?

Of all the questions interviewers ask this is probably the toughest one to answer, because the world is changing so fast. It's hard to know where we'll be one year from now, much less five. There are some good strategies that might help you answer this question. First of all, the real objective behind asking the question is to see whether you have *goals*. The second objective is to get a little insight into your achievement orientation. In other words, do you want to be doing the same thing in five years? Do you want to be promoted? Do you want to be a manager someday? What *are* your aspirations? In addition, this question tests your strategic thinking ability: Have you thought about your career path? Does this job fit into your long-range plans and career goals? Do you genuinely want to learn about and succeed in a particular industry, or do you just see getting a job as a means to pay your rent?

If you have no idea about the future

To answer the question truthfully—especially if you've just graduated from college—you can always qualify your answer. For example, you might say: "I imagine the world will be quite a different place in five years. So, it would be hard for me to know exactly what job I wanted. But there are things I want and expect from my professional life: I would like to keep doing interesting and challenging work. I would like to be recognized for my hard work and promoted to the next level. And I want to continue to build my skills no matter what direction I go in professionally. I'd like to keep learning and growing."

If you know what you want

If you already have a strong sense of what you want to do—if you want to manage people, for example—it's perfectly acceptable to say: "In five years I hope to have some experience at managing a staff." This answer tells the interviewer that you are goal-oriented, set realistic time frames, and prefer a management rather than a technical specialist track. It does not make you sound too eager or pushy.

Starting your own business?

Turnover negatively affects businesses. Between recruiting costs, benefits, and training, your employer has made a significant investment in you and your career. So interviewers are going to try to evaluate how long you will stay with the firm. One way to do that is to ask if you've ever thought about starting your own business.

You will have to be a little savvy about your answer while maintaining integrity. For example, you're interviewing for a job with a technology consulting firm, but you know in the back of your mind that you want to be running your own business in five or six years. It would not be a good idea to say, "I want to get this consulting experience so that I can start my own business." However, it *would* be politically savvy to say, "I'm very interested in learning about consulting and I'd like to work in a broad spectrum of industries." You could even say, "Eventually, I'd like to be a specialist in the technology industry." This answer is not only truthful, it goes a long way toward assuring your prospective employer of three important things: that you are in the right field, that you want to enhance your skills as a consultant, and that you see yourself specializing in a certain area. You've been honest without revealing your ultimate goal, which, eventually, is to leave your employer. But save that conversation for a few years down the road.

Some companies that value innovation may ask, "Did you ever want to start your own company?" These companies want to hire entrepreneurial people who are always thinking of creative products and services. If your answer is "yes," be prepared for a follow-up question that will require you to describe your business idea. Your answer will be evaluated on its uniqueness, its relevance to the marketplace, and how well you've thought it through.

What accomplishment are you most proud of?

Here's another opportunity to talk about your accomplishments in a more personal way than you might have discussed earlier. In this case, you can talk about the most difficult or the most challenging of your work and academic achievements. Or, focus on something that will tell your interviewer something about your values. What do you really care about and admire yourself for doing?

For example, in a recent job interview, John, a sports writer, used the example of finishing the New York City Marathon as his proudest moment. From the outside, John's achievement doesn't appear to be job-related, but if you look at it more closely his story reveals personal qualities that any employer would value in an employee. First of all, completing a marathon requires discipline—it takes months of diligent training to run a 26-mile course. John's story demonstrates an ability to schedule time effectively and focus on achieving a goal. He also shows that he is comfortable with competition—even if that competition is his own best running time. For a prospective employer, these qualities translate into an image of a hard-working and dedicated person who takes pride in his work and would be a valuable addition to the staff.

What would be the ideal company for you?

To prepare for this question, go back to the ten-point chart you made in Chapter 3 and take a look at your list of work requirements. When a prospective employer asks you what kind of a schedule you're looking for or if you're interested in a training program, how will you respond? Do you want to work for a small company or a big one? Do you want client contact or hope to work closely with other team members? Does it matter to you if the company contributes to the community? When an interviewer asks this question, part of the motivation is to discover if you have an interest in the big picture. Will you fit into the larger context? Consider this answer:

> *My ideal job is one that constantly challenges me. I like to be given a variety of projects and handle different kinds of assignments at the same time. I would also like to work in an environment in which initiative is recognized and rewarded. I hope that after proving myself on the job, I will be given new responsibilities.*

This answer demonstrates that the candidate likes to learn new skills, develop new ideas, and take initiative, all of which are valuable characteristics for any employee to have.

Here's another example of a good answer:

> *I want to learn everything there is to know about the pharmaceutical industry. I'm hoping to explore all aspects of the field, from research and development to marketing and consumer trends. The best firm for me would be one that is both innovative and experienced. I don't want to work for a company that refuses to change with the times, but I also think it's important to have a good sense of the past successes and mistakes.*

If you have very specific goals, feel free to express them when answering this question.

What would the ideal boss be like?

We all have different ideas about the boss of our dreams. But nearly anyone could answer truthfully by saying, "A boss I can learn from." You can expand on this by adding, "It would be someone who would let me work independently, but still give me regular feedback." Most organizations want the same thing—bosses who are able to delegate and also give feedback to their employees. Here is another example of a suitable answer:

My ideal boss would be someone who is professional and approachable. Another quality I appreciate and would look for in the ideal boss is the ability to make an employee feel comfortable when she asks questions. I'd also like to receive feedback on my progress—if I'm doing something wrong, I'd like to know about it right away, so I could improve immediately, not six months later after my annual review.

The following tough questions can work for you by prompting specific success stories. When you begin your answer, repeat the question in the form of a statement to help you get your bearings and to add a few more precious moments in which you can mentally compose your answer. Try to choose the closest story you have to match the following common, but more in-depth questions:

1. **Describe a situation where you had a tough decision to make. What did you do? What did you learn? (Decision Making)**
2. **Would you describe yourself as a flexible person? Describe a time when you had to change your direction because you received new information? How did you accomplish this? (Innovative Thinking)**

3. Give an example of how you've discovered appropriate cours-es of action for accomplishing a long-range goal? (Strategic Thinking)

4. What have you done differently from your peers in your class-es/organization? Give an example of what makes you unique. (Accomplishments/Getting Results)

5. Can you give an example of a time when you worked with a group to determine project responsibilities. What was your role? (Team Playing/Team Leadership)

....

Tell me about yourself

This question is sometimes used to open an interview, and part of the motivation behind it is to see what approach the candidate takes. You may choose to give your accomplishments and goals some sort of linear progression, beginning, perhaps, with why you chose your college. Emphasize the thought process that went into your decisions about where you went to college and what you studied and majored in. If you can make a connection between your high school and col-lege ambitions and what you hope to achieve in your career, all the better. On the other hand, you begin with the work experience that has the most relevance to the position for which you're applying.

For some interviewers this is not necessarily a "test" question, but simply a way of starting the conversation and learning as much about you as possible. Then, the information you've volunteered will be the basis of the interviewer's follow-up questions. Here's an example of a positive, thorough response to this type of general question:

After high school, I decided to go to Greer University, because they have an excellent business program. I've always known that I want-ed to go into business, and college seemed like an excellent opportu-nity to give myself a solid background in finance, accounting, and marketing. One of my favorite activities is playing soccer on Greer's varsity soccer team. I spend a lot of time conditioning for the sport and improving my skills. I like pushing myself to meet new challenges, like running more miles or lifting more weight.

This candidate's answer to a general question illustrates the diversity of his interests—not just his ability to work well on a team or focus on goals. The interviewer's follow-up questions to this response might be:

- What influenced your decision to be a business major?
- Give an example of a difficult challenge you faced as a member of the soccer team.
- When you had competing demands between coursework and soccer practice, what did you do?

Who are your heroes?

The point of asking this question is to find out whether you can learn by emulating others, are motivated by others' achievements, and have a standard of excellence for yourself. Your heroes can come from a variety of time periods and sources, such as literature, history and business. You also might choose a parent, family member, or teacher as a hero—personal heroes are just as important as the public figures we admire.

Even more revealing than the people you choose will be your reasons for choosing them, so give some serious thought to the values and traits that make these individuals your heroes. For example, if you say that you admire Thomas Edison because of his creativity as an inventor, an interviewer will get a good sense of your values and, hopefully, how they connect to the company's mission.

Asking about heroes is a good diagnostic tool for an employer. Having heroes demonstrates that you are open to having mentors and receiving guidance from others. It also tells the employer that you will look for successful people in the company and emulate them.

....

Some people say they don't have any heroes because they don't want to be perceived as followers. But that's not what the question "Who are your heroes?" is all about. It's about values and where you want to go with them professionally. It's about corporate hierarchy and whether or not you'll fit in. Every corporation has a hierarchy, and within hierarchies there are heroes. So the question really is: Can you look up to a person within a hierarchy, who has both effective and less effective traits, and extract something to admire, motivate, and inspire you? You may be more comfortable answering the question by choosing two or three traits you admire and then matching a person to each trait.

....

SITUATIONAL OR CASE STUDY QUESTIONS

It is important to familiarize yourself with situational questions, such as: "How many total gallons of gasoline do you think Americans purchase per year?" In most cases, the chances of your being asked this type of question is pretty slim, but it doesn't hurt to be prepared. You will almost certainly have to deal with this sort of question if you are interviewing with consulting firms or financial services companies (investment banks and accounting firms), or if you have graduated from an MBA program. If you fall into one of these categories, see Appendix G for more detailed information on approaching case study questions.

Interviewers sometimes ask situational or case study questions that test critical thinking skills. When faced with one of these questions, the best advice is to think of an *approach* to solving a problem rather than trying to come up with an answer. There are no right or wrong answers to these questions: instead, an interviewer is simply trying to see how you analyze the situation.

Question: How many tons of ketchup do Americans consume every year?

When faced with an out-of-context problem like this, the strategy is to use your analytical skills. Don't just make a wild guess (you don't want your interviewer to think you're comfortable giving out inaccurate information in high-stakes situations). Think about the ways you could approach this problem. You might say that you don't know that answer, but you can think of some good research methods to figure it out. Then describe your methods. You might suggest getting a market report from a major ketchup company, such as Heinz or Hunt's. Market surveys are often included in such reports and might include data on ketchup consumption in the U.S. Or, you might suggest conducting a survey of restaurants and supermarkets across the company. You could then describe how you would plan and implement such a survey.

Or, you might tell the interviewer that you don't know the answer, but that you would be happy to explain how you might go about estimating it. If the interviewer presses for an explanation, you could say:

First, let me think of a small sample size: say, ten of my friends. Six of us like ketchup, and four don't. So, let's assume that 60% of the population likes ketchup. I probably consume five total bottles of ketchup each year, and think that's about average among my friends. Let's say that each bottle contains one pound of ketchup. So, according to my logic, 60 percent of the 250 million people in the United States consume five pounds of ketchup per year. Now, we just have to multiply it out to arrive at an answer.

It is a mistake to treat the question answer flippantly by saying something like, "Actually, I'm a mustard person myself." The interviewer has legitimate reasons for asking the question. If you have no idea how to answer, say so and move on. The trick is to be resilient. Don't let one question throw you. Stay calm so that you can answer the next question.

....

As with all types of questions, the best way to handle case study questions is to be prepared. Talk to the counselors at your college career center or speak with a friend who has case interview experience. There are also a number of good books written on the subject. If you feel you need more practice with this type of question, get a copy of one of these titles:

- *Case Interview: The Vault Reports Guide to the Case Interview*, Mark Asher and Marcy Lerner, Vault Reports, Inc., 1998
- *The Wharton School Case Study Interview Guide* (2 vols.), Wharton MBA Consulting Club, Wet Feet Press, 1997
- *Ace Your Case! The WetFeet.com Essential Management Consulting Case Workbook*, Wet Feet Press, et al., 1998

....

COMMON INTERVIEW QUESTIONS TO CONSIDER

It's impossible to predict or anticipate all the questions that an interviewer will ask. However, it helps to get a sense of the range of questions that might be asked. Below is a list that includes some questions that have already been addressed in these pages, along with quite a few more that are worth considering. These are some of the most common questions asked in interviews. Even if these questions don't come up in your interview, it is a valuable exercise to think about how you might answer them.

If you're stumped, ask a friend to help you. Sometimes it's difficult to pinpoint your own good qualities. An outside point of view is often the best way to gain insight into ourselves.

1. Why are you interested in this field?
2. What was your most challenging or difficult experience?
3. Why did you choose your college?
4. Why did you choose your major in college?
5. What do you know about this firm?
6. Why should I hire you?
7. What qualifications do you have for this job?
8. Describe your ideal job.
9. Describe your ideal boss.
10. Describe your working style.
11. Give an example of a time when you worked in a team. What did you learn?
12. What are your hobbies and interests?
13. How would your friends describe you?
14. How would a teacher describe you?
15. How would a co-worker describe you?
16. What college course did you like the most? Why?
17. What do you think you would like least about this job?
18. What does success mean to you?
19. What would you do if you had a co-worker you didn't get along with?
20. What are some of your pet peeves?
21. Give an example of a challenging problem you had to solve and explain how you came up with your solution.
22. Do you prefer working alone or in teams? Why?
23. Here's a pencil. Sell it to me.
24. What motivates you? What doesn't?
25. Under what conditions do you do your best work?
26. If you had a free afternoon, how would you use your time?
27. How do you define success?
28. What do you think it takes to be successful in this career?
29. Do you have any plans for further education?
30. Have you ever had a conflict with a boss or professor? How did you resolve it?
31. How has your education prepared you for your career?

32. Tell me a little about yourself.
33. How are you different from other candidates interviewing for this position?
34. What are your strengths?
35. What are your weaknesses?
36. Where would you like to be five years from now?
37. Where would you like to be ten years from now?
38. Do you consider yourself a leader? Why or why not?
39. Describe your ideal work environment.
40. What college course did you find the most challenging? Why?
41. Have you ever failed at anything? How did you handle it?
42. What are your long-term career goals?
43. Tell me a story.
44. How do you usually handle conflict with a coworker?
45. What was your greatest disappointment?
46. Describe a time when you were under pressure to perform. What was the outcome?
47. Describe a creative project you were involved in.
48. How would you evaluate your accomplishments so far?
49. Give an example of a time when you had to work independently.
50. What else would you like to tell me about yourself that I don't already know?

GETTING ANOTHER INTERVIEW

If you didn't get the job you wanted, try getting another interview. It can be difficult to negotiate, but there are at least three scenarios where it might be a viable option:

1. **There is another job opening at the company you are interested in.** Joia applied and was interviewed for the position of production assistant at a radio station and didn't get the job. Two weeks later she saw an advertisement in the

Help Wanted section of the newspaper for another position with the same company. This is a perfect example of why it is never a good idea to burn a bridge. Hopefully Joia sent a note to WXRO Radio, thanking them for taking the time to interview her, even though she didn't get the job. If she made a good impression, there's no reason why she shouldn't attempt to go back for another interview. If you were in Joia's position, you should call human resources about the new job listing, try to speak with the same person you worked with the first time around. Tell her how much you enjoyed—and learned from—the last experience, and restate your desire to work for the company. Ask her if you should resubmit your resume and find out if she does or does not recommend that you apply for the new job, given what she already knows about you. This tactic shows that you are very interested in working for the company; your persistence, follow-through, and enthusiasm show the person who is hiring that you have the confidence and initiative necessary to do the job. Joia's persistence paid off. She was better prepared for the second interview and was able to effectively demonstrate that she was the right person to fill the job opening.

Joia Michaels
444 Spring Street
New York, NY 11111
(212) 555–6666
joia@phatpencil.com

May 29, 2000

Joan Blatt
Human Resources Manager
WXRO Broadcasting, Inc.
555 Broadway
New York, NY 11111

Dear Ms. Blatt,

It was a pleasure speaking with you about the position of production assistant at WXRO Broadcasting last week. Although I
was disappointed to learn that you had filled the position,
it has come to my attention that you are now looking for another production assistant. I am still very interested in the
job, and I hope you will reconsider my experience and qualifications. I would greatly appreciate the opportunity to
speak with you again regarding the position.

I truly believe that my strong media background would be a
positive contribution to WXRO Broadcasting, Inc. As we discussed, I produced several regular shows for my college
radio station and spent last summer working as an intern at
Channel 11 News. I am well acquainted with the world of media
communications, and I am confident in my abilities to remain
flexible and organized in this fast-paced field.

I have enclosed another copy of my resume for your review. I
am available for an interview at your convenience. I appreciate your time and consideration in this matter.

Sincerely,

Joia Michaels

Enclosure (1)

2. **You feel that you did poorly in the first interview because of extenuating circumstances.** Dana didn't receive an offer for a second interview either. She hadn't been feeling well because she had a cold. Dana simply called her interviewer the next day to explain that she had not been feeling well and therefore did not feel that she really was able to demonstrate that she was the right fit for the job. Most people are sympathetic to this situation. After some persuasion, Dana convinced her interviewer to schedule another interview. In another scenario, Dana's interview might have been interrupted or cut short unexpectedly. If the interviewer didn't suggest it, Dana should have suggested rescheduling the interview. A potential employer would have appreciated her initiative and continued interest in the job.

3. **You took yourself out of the running but have second thoughts.** Dan was about to receive offers from two different technology firms, EFG.com and lmnopNet. EFG.com was the first company to offer him a job, and their offer included a very generous salary and benefits package. The money was enticing, and Dan decided he would accept the offer. He was scheduled to complete one more round of interviews at lmnopNet, but decided to take himself out of the running for the job. After giving the matter some further thought, Dan realized that his skills and goals were better suited to the job at lmnopNet. When he reevaluated his finances, he figured out cost-cutting measures that would allow him to accept a lower salary. He turned down the EFG.com job and called lmnopNet back. After explaining the situation and reiterating his interest in the job, he persuaded lmnopNet to include him in the next round of interviews.

Thinking on your feet is the crucial ability that will set you apart from other applicants with whom you are competing. Even if you don't believe that you do it well now, it is an ability that you can easily learn. The secret is to be prepared. Although you won't be able to guess exactly what will transpire in every situation, you should do very well in any interview, if you are ready for a variety of questions and have primed several success stories. Look carefully over the questions discussed in this chapter and practice with friends, family members, or any other person you know who has gone through an interview and can offer suggestions. The key is to relax so that you can put your best foot forward and sell yourself to the best of your ability. Remember, most prospective employers ask tough questions because they want to learn about you: what motivates you, where your experience lies, how you will benefit the company, and where you would fit into the company if you were hired. If you answer honestly and thoughtfully, you will be sure to succeed.

ONE ANSWER DOESN'T MAKE OR BREAK AN INTERVIEW

Pearl of Wisdom

"After graduating from college, I interviewed at a large consulting firm. The interviewer asked me how I felt about working on a team. I had several bad experiences working on teams in college. Unlike some of the students I worked with, I set very high standards for myself—so I ended up having to do most of the work myself. With this in mind, I blurted out, 'I don't really enjoy working in team settings.' Working in teams, however, is a very important part of being a consultant, so I quickly added, 'In college, I had some difficulty working on teams. I always set very high standards for myself, and I found it frustrating when other students didn't share my goals. However, I know that things would be different here. Your company is one of the top five consulting firms in the nation, and you set extremely high standards of excellence for your employees. I feel confident that I would work well with the other consultants at this firm. One of the reasons I am interested in working here is to gain more positive experiences working in teams.' Although I initially misspoke, I didn't do myself any real harm. In fact, during the next round of interviews, my interviewer told me that he was impressed with the way I handled myself. I remained professional and unflustered when I made a potentially damaging response, and my explanation demonstrated that I would uphold the firm's high standard of excellence."

—LOUIS, SENIOR CONSULTANT

CHAPTER 8

the job offer

Negotiation Strategies,
When and How to Say "Yes"
and "No" to the Offer

CONGRATULATIONS! YOU'VE BEEN offered the job. . . . Now you have to decide whether or not you want it.

Before you get to yes or no it's important to realize that there is a correlation between how much experience you have and how much negotiating you can do. If you are just beginning your career, there won't be much room to negotiate. But you can strengthen your position if you know exactly how much the job is worth in the open market.

College career fairs probably gave you a good sense of what entry-level salaries are like, but you can always brush up your research skills and do a little investigating on the Internet or at your local library. Most university and big city branches have career-counseling offices in addition to copious reference materials. Many industry associations publish salary surveys. Or, make some calls to people you know who are already working in the business or industry you want to enter. If you got your job through an agency, ask the person you've been working with to advise you.

An important point to remember is that employers who hire a lot of recent college graduates are very savvy about the going rate for jobs. They put an enormous amount of time and money into campus recruiting, so in all likelihood they know even more than you do about the competition and what it can offer. Your best strategy is to look at the whole picture—not just salary—to determine whether a company is for you. For example, Company A may offer less salary than Company B, but perhaps Company A has a much better training program or an attractive bonus arrangement. Know what job features are most important to you and give your priorities the most weight when making your decision.

The truth is that when you are looking for your first job, there is often little room to negotiate a better salary. If you really see yourself working at the company that wants to hire you, don't jeopardize a good job over a few hundred dollars. Having a positive feeling about your workplace is priceless. However, do keep in mind that you must be able to live on your salary (unless you are continuing to live at your parents' home or are otherwise subsidized)—it's very important to do the math while you're deciding whether to accept the job offer. A great idea is to make a list of both the positive and negative sides of the job offer. Be sure to include facts about work environment, salary, benefits, and location; all of these aspects of the job will greatly affect how you feel about your job after the initial "honeymoon period" is over. It is extremely important to make sure that your goals are realistic. Try not to include unreachable goals and desires on your list (a promotion within six months or a six-figure salary, for instance); write down only what you could reasonably attain in your present position.

Sandy, an entry-level interpreter, offers this advice:

Try to create a sample budget. Start with your rent—if you know what you will be paying. Then you'll know the amount of your largest monthly bill. Ideally, your rent should be roughly one-third of your monthly take-home pay. Then there are utilities, such as electric and gas, cable, and phone. (Don't forget to include cellular and ISP charges, if you have these services.) Be mindful of student loans and credit card bills, too. In order to create or maintain good credit, you must pay these bills, in full, each month. Then budget for groceries, transportation, gas, furnishings for a new apartment, entertainment such as movies and dining out, and health insurance co-payments—it all adds up!

Don't forget about taxes. If you are being paid $24,000 a year, do not expect to receive $2,000 every month. Chances are it will be around $1,600. (That's just over $19,000 per year.) Now, deduct all of the monthly estimated bills from your monthly take-home pay. Do you break even? If you're close to a balanced budget, but a bit over on the expenses side, try to trim your entertainment. Recalculate. If the amount you need to spend each month is still not close to your monthly take-home pay, then you have two choices: call to decline the job offer because the salary is too low or find a way to supplement your income.

Lauren, a Web producer, adds this:

Before you throw in the towel, be sure to tell the human resources representative that you're very interested in the job, but that you just can't make it on the offered salary. Add a few comments about how great the prospective team looks to you, and how you really picture yourself in the group. At this point, you've got nothing to lose except the chance at your dream job—inquire about overtime pay or the ability to do freelance assignments, maybe in another department. If there is still no flexibility for greater income, and you really want the job, consider other, part-time work that won't interfere with your career, such as babysitting one or two nights per week, waiting tables on weekends, or working a couple of weekend shifts at the local bookstore or coffee shop. While this is not optimal, you may need to sacrifice some free time to break into certain industries. For example, most media jobs pay very low salaries for entry-level, yet continue to appeal to recent college graduates. For the young, independent folks that seek them, working a couple of nights per week the first year is well worth it. I stuck it out in my industry, and I often look back on the nights waiting tables, copy-editing, and tutoring as equally valuable training. I worked hard, balanced my budget, and even saved money to go on some great vacations. Just remember not to take on too much outside work—you don't want your boss to think that you're too tired at the start of your "real" job on Monday mornings.

Keep in mind, you'll need to balance salary requirements with other aspects of the job opportunity. During the research phase of your job search, find out other positive qualities of a company. When you zero in on a job in a company that you really like, keep in mind that you'll be spending at least 40 hours per week at this office. You'll want to be doing work that challenges you, with people you like and can learn from. If these factors are sufficiently appealing at a particular company, chances are the financial issues will work out for you, too.

....

If there is something about a job offer that doesn't meet your expectations, bring it up *as soon as* you get the offer, rather than waiting for two or three days to say there's something on your mind. If you wait—and make people at the company wait—they'll be less likely to negotiate.

....

NEGOTIATING TIPS
FOR MORE EXPERIENCED JOB HUNTERS

If you've had some solid work experience, it is possible to negotiate your salary based on three variables:

1. *Your total compensation package at your current job.* This includes your base salary, bonuses, and benefits, such as company contribution to a 401(k) plan. In some cases, your new employer may want you to start working before you receive your bonus at your current job. Your employer may be willing to pay you the amount of the bonus in order to get you to start by a certain date.

2. *Specialized skills or experience.* Let's say you're going to work for a technology company and have a great deal of experience in computer programming. Your new employer may be willing to pay for your expert skills. Or, if you've worked for a large consulting firm and are now going to work for a boutique firm, your new employer may be willing to increase your salary because you bring broad experience to the firm. Fluency in foreign languages, computer savvy, and knowledge of any specialized field are all marketable skills.

3. *Salary benchmarking.* Every job has a certain salary range. It's your job to find out that range through networking and other methods of research (described in Chapter 3). If your prospective employer offers a salary lower than the going rate, you can say, "Based on my research, comparable positions in other firms are starting at X salary. I feel that I should be compensated similarly."

WHEN AND HOW TO SAY YES TO THE JOB OFFER

As much as you might want to say "Yes!" to a job the minute it is offered, it is wiser to wait, even if you're sure you want the job. First of all, take a deep breath and thank the person who called you with the good news. Tell him or her that you're thrilled and excited about the job offer but need a day to think it over. This is an accepted protocol: It is perfectly all right to ask the person who has extended a job offer to wait twenty-four hours for your answer. However, it is completely unacceptable to keep him or her waiting for a week. If you get a job offer on a Friday, say that you will call back on Monday with your answer. But if you get an offer on Monday, you should reply on Tuesday, unless you have not received certain information you requested, such as a written job offer or a letter outlining the benefits package.

In the twenty-four hours you have to consider whether you want a job—and even if you *are* sure you want it—there are a few things you need to do:

1. Review the chart you made in Chapter 3 that lists the ten factors that must be satisfied before you will accept a job— just to make sure that you haven't overlooked anything. Is there anything the job is not offering you that you wished it had? And of the things you're not going to get, are any of them deal breakers?
2. Is there a way to negotiate getting some of the things you want?
3. Before you go too far with your plans, ask a mentor, parent, or friend to act as a sounding board.

Take this time to think about the interviews you've had with the company. If you've established a good rapport with your interviewer, it's easy to overlook certain points. Before saying yes to a job, make sure you know what the specifics are about the following:

- **Annual salary:** What are you paid and how often? When will you be eligible for raises or promotions? What is the typical salary increase?
- **Benefits:** What the company covers (i.e. medical and dental

coverage, etc.), when you are eligible, and how much money, if any, is deducted from paychecks to cover benefits. Also, ask if preexisting medical conditions exclude you from coverage for a certain period.

- **Other Perks:** Vacations, holidays, sick or personal days, 401(k) plans, stock options, funding for commuting or tuition/education expenses, health club memberships, etc.
- **Bonuses:** Are there incentive programs or holiday bonuses? By what date do you have to start to be eligible for them?
- **Job title:** What is your job description—assistant, intern, or coordinator? To whom will you report?
- **Performance assessment:** When the company reviews your job performance: one year after your start date or at a scheduled time every year? Who will write your review? What is a typical percent of salary increase for this level?
- **Start date:** Get the exact day and date, as well as starting time.
- **To whom do you report?** It may not be the person who hired you, but rather an associate manager.

At first glance, the job specifics listed above may seem obvious to you, but do yourself a favor and double-check with your contact at the company. Company protocol often dictates that you receive an offer letter stating the conditions of your employment. If something is missing from the letter, especially something that was promised verbally, ask that you receive a new letter or addendum.

Claire, a New York publicist, had a great interview with a company based in Los Angeles. At the second interview, salary, job title, and benefits were discussed. In fact, she was offered the position of senior publicist for a branch office that was scheduled to open in New York sometime in the near future. Claire accepted the job, which was offered by her prospective supervisor, a vice president with the company. Based on that meeting, she gave notice at her current job, and then made plans to start with the company at their New York office. However, there was one enormous snag: The opening of the New York office was postponed for almost four months!

Although Claire's supervisor—the man who offered her the job—was the VP in charge of hiring, he was not in charge of deciding *when* the New York office would be launched. Because of this unfortunate timing and her reluctance to clarify the terms of her employment, Claire was left without a job, waiting for her employment to begin. It is vitally important to know all the specifics before accepting a job, especially details as basic as your start date.

It's perfectly acceptable to negotiate salary, vacation, etc. with a company. But be careful about asking for too much—your judgment and maturity might be questioned and you could be perceived as someone whose expectations will always be higher than what the employer can deliver. Do your research and base your expectations on the normal compensation of a person in your position with this prospective employer.

KNOWING WHAT YOU WANT

In today's fast-paced economy, it is not uncommon to receive multiple job offers. Getting more than one offer at the same time is heady stuff, but it can be confusing if you aren't completely sure what you want. If you get flustered and make a wrong decision or say the wrong thing, don't panic. It *isn't* impossible to do a little damage control. But first you need to decide which job you really want. For example, say you've interviewed with two companies: Company A and Company B. You really want to work for Company A, but you get an offer from Company B first. In your excitement, you call Company A and inform them that you've had an offer from another company. You tell them that the "other" company wants your answer by Friday. Then, you ask Company A to give you *their* answer by Friday. You are promptly told that a decision cannot be made by Friday because the decision-makers are in Europe and will not be back until the following week. At this point you don't know what to say. Maybe you're suddenly overwhelmed with doubts that if you don't say yes to Company B on Friday, you'll end up without a job. After all, even if you wait you may be turned down by Company A. Out of panic you say, "Well, I guess you should take me out of the running." Or perhaps Company A takes the initiative and says, "In that case, we're going to have to take you out of the running." As you hang up the phone, you realize—with a sinking feeling—that something really bad has happened. Now what?

Honesty is the best policy

After a little honest self-appraisal, you realize that you do not want to work for Company B *at all,* and that it was probably a bad idea to put pressure on Company A to give you an answer by Friday.

The next morning you call Company A, apologize for pressuring them for an answer, and tell them that you've re-thought the situation. You go on to say that the job with Company A is a much better opportunity than the one offered by "the other company," and that you are willing to wait for Company A to make their decision. At that point your name is put back on the list.

Initially, you may have made a mistake with Company A, but ultimately their decision-making about you will be positively influenced by these factors:

- You really want to work for the company
- You are willing to turn down a sure thing—an offer from another company—just to stay in the running
- You are honest
- You take initiative
- You take risks to get the things you want

You should also keep in mind that many firms will be somewhat flexible about the amount of time you will be given to make a decision. In the scenario above, it would be perfectly acceptable to call

Company B and explain the situation. Say that you are waiting to hear from another company, and, although you remain very enthusiastic about their offer, you want to be able to consider all of your options before making such a big decision. You are demonstrating to Company B that you are a careful and prudent decision-maker. And the very worst that can happen is that you will not be given an extension—in which case you are no worse off than you were before.

GETTING WHAT YOU WANT

Finally, you've received the call you've been waiting for, and you can't believe the offer is for real—until your contact at the company starts talking about money. You've already stated what you want to make as a salary, but now the company is offering an amount that is much less than you expected. The feelings of euphoria you felt earlier vanish altogether when your contact tells you that there's absolutely no flexibility where salary is concerned. When you ask why, he very reasonably explains that there are people in the department who have more experience than you, and who have worked there longer. If the company paid you more, there would be a salary inequity. Clearly, there's no room for negotiation.

Making less than you had anticipated is a setback. But, as you've read earlier in this chapter, there are very good reasons for taking a job anyway—especially if it's the job you want and the company offers other compensation enhancers, such as stock options, health club memberships, or funding for extra training or education. If your salary will be a little less than you'd counted on, consider asking about some of the following forms of compensation:

- Would you be able to negotiate an earlier performance review, say after six months?
- Would you be able to start with a sign-on bonus?
- If you are relocating, would the company be willing to help with some moving costs?

There are two reasons why the company might be willing to give you funds, other than salary, for any of the above:

- When you are paid a salary, the company is actually spending more money than you are getting as salary because it has to add on payroll taxes, benefits costs, and various other expenses involved in keeping you on the payroll.
- One-time payments such as relocation costs and sign-on bonuses usually come out of another part of the company budget—not salary.

Here is an example of a tactful, yet effective strategy to negotiate a little more, if the salary you are offered is lower than you expected and lower than you can live on:

Candidate: I am extremely interested in working with you and your company. Unfortunately, I cannot accept your offer at this point, because the salary will not allow me to move from San Diego to New York City. If you were able to offer an 8 percent salary increase and pay a portion of my relocation expenses, I would gladly accept the position immediately.

In this scenario, the candidate clearly demonstrates his interest in the offered job, but also makes it perfectly clear that he needs more from the company. He has thoroughly considered the job offer from every angle, and he has opened the doors of communication firmly, but professionally.

STARTING WHEN YOU WANT TO START

Here's another scenario: You graduated in May, spent a tough summer doing nothing but interviewing, and haven't had any time off. Not only are you exhausted, but you haven't had time to furnish your new apartment, buy a computer, etc. You secured a job in the fall and the company wants you to start right away. You want to start right away, too, but you'd also like some time off in the next few months. However, the company's vacation policy states that you can't take any time off until you've been with the company for at least one year. What can you do? Before you give up on taking a break, consider these options:

- Tell the truth. You've worked hard during your job search and you plan to give 100 percent to your new job. You'd like some time off before you start to get reenergized and take care of some personal business. Give your employer a specific start date.
- Tell the company you're willing to start work when they want you to, but ask if you could take a week off without pay sometime in the first few months. Give the company a specific time when you want to be away so that everyone can plan for your absence.
- If you are moving from another city, say that you need some time to move and take care of other relocation matters. State the date that you'd like to start.
- If you have planned a vacation for some time in the future, be sure to mention it during the salary negotiation stage. It's a mistake to accept the position and then tell your boss three months later that you need some time off. Be prepared to take the time off without pay, if necessary.

Be flexible. A recent graduate who accepted a position as a marketing specialist asked to delay her start date by a week. As it turned out, her new company was having its annual marketing meeting during that week. She knew it would send the wrong signal if she missed the meeting, so she asked if she could attend the meeting but make her official start date a week later. The company appreciated her willingness to adjust her plans to meet a business need and granted her the time off.

• •

It is common practice to take a few days before starting a new job. If an employer asks why you need the time, here are a few perfectly legitimate reasons:

- You need to finish out a temporary job
- You want to get doctors' appointments out of the way so that you won't need to take time off once you start
- You have to attend to various personal needs/errands addressed (i.e. business clothes shopping, getting a phone line for your new apartment, working out details of your commute, etc.)

• •

ANNOUNCING YOUR NEW JOB

Now that you've started a new job, you need to let everyone in your network know what company you're working for, what your position is, and how you can be contacted. Thank them again for their help during your job search. Send the good news on company letterhead the first week on the job. Or, it is equally appropriate to do this via e-mail from your new company. Be sure to include everyone you talked to about finding a job—whether it was a recruiter, a networking contact, or a college chum. Also, it's appropriate to write a couple lines about the projects you hope to be working on, i.e. "refining the mission of the global marketing team." If you don't use company stationery, use plain, good quality writing paper and be sure to include your work address and phone number. The following is a sample announcement letter:

William White
www.zeemag.com
555 Green Street
New York, NY 11111
(212) 555–5555
ww@zeemag.com

May 28, 2000

Dear Friends,

Now that I have officially signed on the dotted line, I'm pleased to let you know that I have decided to join *Z Magazine, Inc.*, a leading entertainment publication, as associate marketing manager of its online magazine, zeemag.com. I am looking forward to joining this new and exciting group. I want to thank all of you for your support and advice over the last few months.

I will be working with my boss in building affinity partnerships with other companies in Web entertainment, which will be a new area of growth for me. And, I'll be working on promotions and publicity for zeemag's new e-newsletter, *Daily Z*, which is launching this summer.

I hope to talk to you soon. In the meantime, please visit our website at www.zeemag.com.

Regards,

Will

Staying in touch with your network

The importance of staying in touch with the people in your network cannot be emphasized enough. They are the lifeblood of the business world and will help provide you with information, support, and jobs throughout your career. The mistake that even the most senior executives make is to be so focused on their new job that they forget to stay in touch with their network.

You will also want to spend time expanding your network as you look for role models and mentors. If your boss gives you an assignment and you really don't know where to start, you'll always have the option of going to your network for help.

SAYING NO TO AN OFFER

Be very diplomatic about turning down an offer. You certainly don't want to burn any bridges or alienate anyone, particularly since you never know when you might be meeting or working with the same people.

Being gracious

Declining an offer graciously is standard professional behavior. Respond to the offer quickly. You have to draw a clear line about when you have enough data to accept a job or decline it. Once you've made that decision, follow through.

If it turns out that you don't want the job, the first thing to do is to say something positive. For example, "I enjoyed meeting you and I appreciate the time you spent with me." Next, it's important to give a real reason for not taking the job. You might say something along these lines (if applicable), "However, I am declining your offer because at this point in my career, I think I would be better off with a company that offers me a structured training program." This is not the time to give the company negative feedback. You want to preserve your network.

If the real reason for not accepting an offer has to do with salary, go ahead and say so. You might be surprised by the results. Sometimes an employer will offer you more money if you have to turn down a job because of salary concerns. And it's not unheard of for an employer to increase your salary if she really wants you.

When considering the salary offer, remember to factor in the cost of benefits provided. Health insurance (and dental, vision, and mental health coverage) is very expensive. It's common for companies to have a policy on a "probationary period," such as three months, before you receive benefits. Some companies' benefits begin on day one, while others make you wait a whole year before coverage begins. Know your options. Can you secure coverage under your parents' plan until you have benefits? Can you afford to buy your own health care coverage until your company's policy starts? Don't forget, benefits may also include 401(k) plans, stock options, and a vacation/holiday package. These are big issues. If a company offers little to no coverage, it can be a bad sign, and possibly a signal to keep looking. Deduct your out-of-pocket expenses from the offered salary before making a decision.

Even if you do not have another offer, you should decline an offer that doesn't meet your needs as courteously as possible. You might say you're turning down the job because you've decided to investigate another aspect of the field, or perhaps you want to get another kind of experience altogether, such as graduate school. But the most important thing is to make the call. It will be one of the first tests of your mettle as a business person, so do it on time, do it pleasantly and thank the person for their offer and their time. Before you hang up say something reinforcing about the company such as: "I enjoyed meeting you and your management team. Speaking with you taught me a great deal about Internet commerce."

Taking a job you don't want

You may be tempted to accept a job offer for a job that you're not interested in because you don't have any other offers. Don't do it. Your new employer has every reason to expect that you will give 100 percent to your new job. After all, you did everything possible in the interview process to prove that you were a committed and enthusiastic candidate. If you're not willing to make good on your promises, it's not ethical to take the job. In addition, it will be much more difficult to look for another job once you're employed. Finding a job is a full-time job in itself, and you will have much less time and flexibility. If you've gotten disappointing results from your search, analyze what you've been doing and figure out what you could do differently. Brainstorm, and you may find that you have not tapped all your resources.

No matter what you decide to do about negotiating the terms of a new job, you now know the steps to take as well as the protocol. You know that you should really weigh your options before you make a final decision or take any action. All of your research concerning the job market and the details of your particular industry has prepared you for this final step in the interview process. Hopefully, you have made a realistic decision about what you want and what you can attain, given your experience and background. Remember that part of negotiating is making sure that you have all the facts you need to make a decision; and once the offer has been made *you* have to decide whether or not to accept it.

PUTTING IT ALL TOGETHER

Job hunting doesn't have to be a stressful experience. By now you have learned that the process is manageable—and even enjoyable at times—if you do a little planning and inform yourself along the way.

This book offers all the tools and advice you need to feel in charge of your job hunt and find the position you want.

Chapter 1 helps you get your job search started. This chapter explains the best places to find job openings—from help wanted ads in your local paper to the Internet and beyond. But no search is complete without involving the people in your network. Chapter 1 teaches you how to build and maintain a network of contacts—people who are already in the working world and who can help you find out more about the field or job that interests you. Very often it is a contact in your network who helps arrange your first job interview. Nurture your network because, as you will soon discover, it is the most valuable resource you have.

Chapter 2 shows how to write an effective resume and cover letter. These documents are the equivalent of a professional calling card: You can't get a foot in the door without one. Your resume and cover letter give a potential employer his first impression of you, so you'll want to be sure that it is a good one. Although there are dozens of ways to write a resume, the most effective approach utilizes the P-A-R format. Chapter 2 shows you how to put the format to work by translating your educational background and work experiences (no matter how marginal they may seem to you) into a showcase for your skills and accomplishments. At the same time you will learn how to craft a cover letter that highlights your achievements and communicates your enthusiasm and qualifications for a job.

Before an interview, take the time to research a company as thoroughly as you can. Chapter 3 looks at how to investigate the job market, research a company and get information on a job before you interview. But there's one more important area you need to research before you walk into an interview with complete self-assurance: yourself. Now is the time to give careful thought not only to what *you* want from a job but what you can contribute to it. Think about your past accomplishments in terms of how they might fit the requirements of a job. How can your experiences be translated into marketable skills? Other than your educational background, work, or specialized training, what are your best qualities, talents, and gifts, and how can they contribute to a job or a company? Chapter 4 helps you focus your thoughts around Ten Success Factors that every potential employer looks for in a job candidate.

In Chapter 4, we also show you how to link these Ten Success Factors, such as "initiative," "team playing," or "decision making," with your own success stories. You want to *illustrate* your accomplishments rather than list or report them as facts. You are much more convincing and give far greater proof of your claims if you can tell illustrative stories about your skills and accomplishments. In Chapter 4 you learn how to write, rehearse, and tell your "Success Stories" to maximum effect when you need them.

Arriving for an interview with a well-written resume, information about the company, and a number of convincing success stories is your foundation for a great interview, but you also need to focus on your presentation. Do you know what to wear to an interview? Do you have any idea how to read your interviewer's body language or what she might be reading into yours? Relax! Chapter 4 discusses how to stay cool and look professional at all times. There are tips about what to wear, how to build rapport with your interviewer, how to listen, and how to read and send nonverbal signals. Feeling polished and looking your best will give you a tremendous sense of self-assurance.

After your interview, you'll need to follow up to show your interest and stay fresh in your interviewer's mind. There is a recipe for "following up"—and courtesy is the key ingredient. One of the most important aspects of getting and keeping a job is anticipating and satisfying the needs and expectations of others. Courtesy is a powerful form of showing your respect for other people and what they have done for you. Writing a thank-you note to your interviewer is the ideal (and expected) mode of expressing your appreciation. Even if you left your interviewer with a good impression of your personality and qualifications for the job, it won't be enough if you don't follow-up with a well-written thank-you note. If you have any doubts about how to write one, Chapter 4 has solid examples. There is also plenty of information about how to evaluate whether a job is right for you, based on information gleaned from the interview as well as your own criteria for the ideal job.

One of the most difficult aspects of being interviewed for the first time is not knowing what to expect. If you don't know what the difference is between an informational interview and a panel interview, or if you've never even heard of a case interview, Chapters 5 and 6 will guide you through every variety and permutation. Through helpful interview scenarios you will learn how to put your success stories to work. These pivotal chapters demonstrate the skill of interweaving your work and life experiences with the requirements of a job, and showing how your qualifications match them. And, of course, there's plenty of information about the etiquette of interviewing offsite or on campus, and how to follow up any interview effectively and courteously.

Part of gaining confidence in yourself is knowing how to troubleshoot. In other words: How to anticipate problems before they happen. Now that you know how to mobilize your success stories in order to show your talents in the best light, you need to know what types of questions you will be asked and the best way to answer them. Chapter 7 provides a road map that will show you where all the pitfalls, hairpin curves and detours are. You'll find information about how to handle surprise questions and tricky questions and how to get unstuck when an interview goes off course. And there's plenty of advice about answering tough questions. There is even a list of the top 25 mistakes candidates make and how to avoid them, as well as an additional list of the most commonly asked interview questions.

The secret to a successful interview is learning how to participate actively in the interview process. Don't take a passive stance and expect your interviewer to do all the work. Unfortunately, some are less skilled than others about asking questions and guiding the conversation toward a satisfying end. The question in your mind should always be, "How can I make this interview a great interview?" Usually there's something more you can do if you really want a job. Chapter 7 tells you about some of your options, including how to follow-up if you need a second interview and how to correct an interview mistake or a misstatement in a thank-you note.

Finally, Chapter 8 brings you to the conclusion of all of your research, networking, resume-mastery, good listening, good story-telling, and trouble-shooting: a job offer. Now you need to figure out whether you want the job—and how to negotiate the best terms and accept an offer, if you do. It all sounds so easy, but it's important to learn when to say yes and how to decline a job offer graciously. Chapter 8 offers strategies to compensate for a salary that is less than you wanted and suggests questions to ask a prospective employer to give you more options. Finally, there's useful information about formalizing an offer and writing an announcement letter to tell everyone you know about your good fortune.

This book ends where it began: with your network. Don't forget the people who helped you get where you are. They will continue to be your most important resource, not just for the first job, but also for the next and all the ones to follow. But right now it's time to get to work. Good luck and enjoy your new job!

Pearl of Wisdom

TAKE SOME TIME TO THINK ABOUT THE FIELD IN WHICH YOU WANT TO WORK AND THE KIND OF JOB YOU REALLY WANT.

"I interviewed a young woman who had applied for a sales position. As soon as we started talking, I could tell she wasn't right for the job. She was shy and soft-spoken, she hated talking to strangers on the phone, and she liked working independently, rather than on teams. I was very curious why she was interviewing for a sales job, and I pushed her for more information: it turned out that her parents had encouraged her to go into sales, although she was more interested in a job in research. It was obvious she wasn't that interested in, or well suited

for, the job, so I told her she was wasting her time interviewing for sales positions. I think it's extremely important that all job hunters put a lot of time and thought
into deciding what types of jobs interest them and where
their skills and qualifications will take them. If you look
for jobs in a field you don't like or know nothing about,
you'll only be wasting your time and the interviewer's
time."

—Eli, Marketing Executive

ⒶⓅⓅⒺⓃⒹⒾⓍ **A**

print resources

101 Great Answers to the Toughest Interview Questions. Ronald W. Fry, Career Press, 2000.

101 Ways to Power Up Your Job Search. J. Thomas Buck, William R. Matthews, and Robert M. Leech, McGraw-Hill, 1997.

The 250 Job Interview Questions You'll Most Likely Be Asked . . . and the Answers That Will Get You Hired! Peter Veruki, Adams Media Corporation, 1999.

60 Seconds and You're Hired. Robin Ryan, Penguin USA, 2000.

Ace Your Case!: The WetFeet.com Essential Management Consulting Case Workbook. Wet Feet Press, 1998.

Best Jobs for the 21st Century for College Graduates. J. Michael Farr and LaVerne L. Ludden, JIST Publishing, 2000.

Can You Start Monday? A 9–Step Job Search Guide . . . Resume to Interview. Cheryl A. Cage et al., eds., Cage Consulting, Inc., 1998.

Case Interview: The Vault Reports Guide to the Case Interview. Mark Asher and Marcy Lerner, Vault Reports, Inc., 1998.

Cliffs Notes: Delivering a Winning Job Interview. Mercedes Bailey, IDG Books-Cliffs Notes, 2000.

College Grad Job Hunter: Insider Techniques and Tactics for Finding a Top-Paying Entry Level Job. Brian D. Krueger, Adams Media Corporation, 1998.

The Complete Idiot's Guide to the Perfect Interview. Marc Dorio and William Myers, Alpha Books, 2000.

The Complete Professional. Brigit Dermott, ed., LearningExpress, 2000.

The Complete Q&A Job Interview Book. Jeffrey G. Allen, John Wiley & Sons, 1997.

The Complete Resume and Job Search Book for College Students. Bob Adams, Adams Media Corporation, 1999.

Cover Letters That Knock 'Em Dead. Martin J. Yate, Adams Media Corporation, 1998.

Effective Business Speaking. Judith A. McManus, LearningExpress, 1999.

Electronic Resumes: A Complete Guide to Putting Your Resume On-Line. James C. Gonyear and Wayne M. Gonyear, McGraw-Hill, 1996.

Electronic Resumes & Online Networking. Rebecca Smith, Career Press, 1999.

The Everything Resume Book. Steven Graber, Adams Media Corporation, 2000.

The Fool-Proof Job Search Workbook. Donald Asher, Ten Speed Press, 1999.

Getting Interviews. Kate Wendleton, Career Press, 2000.

Great Resume. Jason R. Rich, LearningExpress, 2000.

High Impact Resumes and Letters: How to Communicate Your Qualifications to Employers (7th Edition). Ronald L. Krannich, Impact Publications, 1998.

How to Have a Winning Job Interview. Deborah Perlmutter Bloch, VGM Career Horizons, 1998.

Improve Your Writing for Work, 2nd Edition. Elizabeth Chesla, LearningExpress, 2000.

Interview for Success: A Practical Guide to Increasing Job Interviews, Offers, and Salaries. Cheryl Rae Krannich and Ronald L. Krannich, Impact Publications, 1998.

Interview Power: Selling Yourself Face to Face. Tom Washington, Mount Vernon Press, 2000.

Interview Strategies That Lead to Job Offers. Marilyn Pincus, Barron's, 1999.

Job Interviewing for College Students. John D. Singleton, VGM Career Horizons, 1996.

Job Interviews for Dummies. Joyce Lain Kennedy, IDG Books Worldwide, 1999.

Landing the Job You Want: How to Have the Best Job Interview of Your Life. William C. Byham, Debra Pickett, contributor, Three Rivers Press, 1999.

Networking for Novices. Susan Shelley, LearningExpress, 1999.

Power Interviews: Job-Winning Tactics from Fortune 500 Recruiters. Neil M. Yeager, Lee Hough, contributor, John Wiley & Sons, 1998.

Resume Catalog: 200 Damn Good Examples. Yana Parker, Ten Speed Press, 1997.

Search Smart and Get Ahead. Susan Shelly, LearningExpress, 2000.

The Unofficial Guide to Acing the Interview. Michelle Tullier, Unofficial Panel, ed., IDG Books Worldwide, 1999.

The Wharton School Case Study Interview Guide, 2 vols. Wharton MBA Consulting Club, Wet Feet Press, 1997.

What Color Is Your Parachute? 2000. Richard Nelson Bolles, Ten Speed Press, 1999.

Why Should I Hire You? Turn Interview Questions into Job Offers. J. Michael Farr and Susan Christophersen, JIST Works, 1999.

You're Hired! Secrets to Successful Job Interviews. Sharon McDonnell, IDG Books Worldwide, 1999

online resources

JOB SEARCH SITES

(starred sites are recommended by LearningExpress)

www.123-job.com

www.careercity.com

www.careermart.com

* www.careermosaic.com

* www.collegegrad.com

www.govtjobs.com

* www.headhunter.net

* www.hotjobs.com

www.iamag.com/infoage/virtual.htm ("The Virtual Recruiting Network")

www.jobs.com

www.jobsonline.com

www.jobs-network.com

www.jobvault.com

* www.monster.com

www.vault.com

RESOURCE SITES

www.amazon.com	books
www.careers.yahoo.com	information and links
www.dse.state.mn.us/cjs/cjs_site	Minnesota Dept. of Economic Security; resources, etc.
www.garywill.com/worksearch	information and links to resources
www.jobinterview.net	mock interviews, sample questions, books, etc.
www.provenresumes.com	resume tips and strategies, bookstore, etc.
www.student.com/jobs	stories, bulletin boards, job ideas, etc.
www.careers.yahoo.com/employment/ research/salaries_benefits	salary calculator
www.view.womenswire.com/work/ toolkit.html	job hunting tips for women

APPENDIX C

sample resumes

Resume 1: Alexander J. Simms

Resume 2: Alice P. Kaper

Alexander J. Simms

PO Box 114817, La Jolla, CA 55870   e-mail: alex.simms@lju.edu   544–555–0710
14 Sunshine Drive, Fresno, CA 55791   351–555–2743

EDUCATION   **La Jolla University, La Jolla, CA**
BS, Molecular Biophysics & Biochemistry and Economics, May 1999
GPA: 3.75

Academic Honors and Awards
William T. Marlowe Scholarship for Excellence in National
Environmental Policy, 1998
Hastings Summer Fellowship, 1998
Dean's Prize in Biochemistry

EXPERIENCE   **LJU Center for Environmental Law and Policy**   1997–Present
*Director, Trade and Environment in the Latin America Project
(1998–Present)*
Responsible for researching and developing an action agenda to
address trade and environment concerns in Western Hemisphere
free trade negotiations. This includes economic analysis, policy evaluation, interviews with U.S. and foreign officials and experts,
research, and writing reports.
• Co-authored with Marcos Santiago a forthcoming book:
  Environmental Protection and Globalization in Latin America.
• Presented at 1997 World Environment and Trade conference in
  Washington, DC attended by over 100 politicians, business leaders, and scholars from the United States and Latin America.

Research Associate, Brazilian Environment Project (Summer 1997)
• Conducted research and assisted in writing of Gold and Green:
  Trade and the Environment in Twentieth-Century Brazil (Harper
  University Press, 1998).

Los Angeles Academy of Sciences, Los Angeles, CA   Summer, 1998
Research Associate, Los Angeles Cancer Research Foundation
Responsible for researching issues in patent law and biotechnology.
• Prepared report on national sources of cancer research funding by
  compiling data from government agencies, pharmaceutical companies, and philanthropies, resulting in a 15% increase in requests for
  proposals.
• Presented findings at California Cancer Research Foundation
  meeting attended by policymakers, scientists, physicians, and
  healthcare industry professionals.

South Bay Harbor Laboratory,   1993–1995, Summer 1996
South Bay Harbor, CA
Student Researcher, Dr. Ellen Richardson's laboratory
Responsible for laboratory research in cancer cell biology, cancer
genetics, and human genome mapping.
• Developed new technique for long-range genetic mapping.

ACTIVITIES/ **LEADERSHIP**	**La Jolla University Debate Association** *Vice President, current; 1997 La Jolla Invitational Tournament Director* • Intercollegiate parliamentary debate team, competing regionally and nationally
	LJU Weekly News *Columnist and News Editor* • Editorial and production responsibilities include managing staff, layout and design, investigative reporting, and writing weekly op-ed column on international affairs.
INTERESTS	Intramural sports (tennis, track and field); jogging; music (piano and flute); proficient in Spanish

---

REFERENCES AVAILABLE UPON REQUEST

Note: Because the page size of this book is smaller than the standard 8½" x 11" resume page, this sample is set as two pages. Your resume should be one page.

Alice P. Kaper

41 West Fourth Street, Apt. 5F
New York, NY 12908

akaper@iweb.com
(212) 555-2981

EDUCATION

Blake University, New Haven, CT
BA, Magna Cum Laude. Major in English.
Phi Beta Kappa, George Hastings English Prize

William Greer Centre, London, England
Blake-in-London Program, Fall 1997

EXPERIENCE

Slate & Fisher, New York, NY   June 1999–present
Legal Assistant
Responsible for the organization and maintenance of case files.
Perform general clerical duties. Assist attorneys in trial preparation
and at trial.
- Recognized for strong organizational skills, computer knowledge,
  and ability to manage multiple tasks under extreme time pressures.
- Received Defense Attorneys' Association award for outstanding
  pro bono service.

Dr. Emma Benning, English Dept., New Haven, CT   1997–1999
Research Assistant
Tasks included research, proofreading and editing manuscripts, and
selecting material to be used in scholarly criticism.
- Utilized on-line databases and foreign language sources to conduct extensive library research, facilitating Dr. Bennington's publication of three articles in scholarly journals.

Blake Center for Advanced Research, New Haven, CT   1996–1997
Office Assistant
Performed clerical duties, including research and file management,
in the Learning and Attention Department of a premier research
institute.
- Designed and published newsletter using Microsoft Publisher;
  contributed three articles on dyslexia and learning disabilities.
- Constructed and managed databases using Microsoft Access to
  ensure efficient access to research materials.

Blake University Dean's Office, New Haven, CT   1995–1996
Office Assistant
Duties included composing fundraising letters, answering phones,
and managing files.
- Managed the Blake peer tutoring program and increased visibility
  of the program through direct mail campaign resulting in a 20%
  increase in peer tutor volunteers.

Office of Dr. Alan Janovich, M.D., New York, NY   Summer 1996
Office Assistant
Responsible for clerical duties, including answering phones, scheduling appointments and billing. Coded and completed health insurance claim forms.
- Improved office customer service by serving as a liaison between
  doctor and patient.

ACTIVITIES

P.A.T.H. Peer Counseling, Publicity Coordinator, 1996–1997
Blake Literary Magazine, Managing Editor, 1998–1999
Hartley Children's Hospital, Volunteer

A P P E N D I X D

sample letters

April 3, 2000

Pearl Usher
Senior Recruiting Administrator
Prynne & Company, Inc.
211 West Hawthorne Street
Dimsdale, MA 52660

Dear Ms. Usher:

I would like to be considered for the Business Analyst position at Prynne & Company, Inc. I am currently a senior at Giles University, and will graduate in May with a degree in Economics. Through my coursework in this field and my experience at the National Economic Research Foundation, I have honed my research skills and gained exposure to different styles of problem solving and analysis-skills which I believe are well-suited to management consulting.

For four years, I have been actively involved in *The Giles Herald*, a weekly campus newspaper. As the current Managing Editor, it is my responsibility to turn a 75-person staff into a high-performance team to produce 28 pages of news, sports, opinion, and arts each week. I have also been an active member of the debate team, an activity which has helped me develop excellent speaking and communication skills.

I enclose a resume, and look forward to the opportunity to discuss my experience and qualifications in an interview. Thank you for your consideration.

Sincerely,

Amelia S. Chen
PO Box 4590
West River, MA 40028
514-555-0632
amelia.chen@giles.edu

June 16, 2000

R. John Thurston
Human Resources Director
Pimm Publishing
4650 Goldenrod Avenue
Austin, TX 77011

Dear Mr. Thurston:

I am writing to apply for the position of editorial assistant, which I saw advertised in the *Austin Daily News*. I am a recent graduate of Pierce College, where I received a degree in English. I graduated magna cum laude, and received the Thornton-Wesley Prize for outstanding achievement in writing.

As an English major, I developed excellent written and verbal communication skills, and I honed these skills while serving on the staff of the *Pierce Literary Magazine*. I have also spent three years working as a Pierce Computer Assistant; as a CA, I received extensive training in a variety of computer programs, including Microsoft Office, PowerPoint, Adobe Illustrator, Quark, and Photoshop. Finally, I spent last summer working at Gulliver Publications, where I learned the intricacies of the publishing industry.

I believe that my skills and experiences have prepared me for a job at Pimm Publishing. I am confident that my organizational skills, diligence, and enthusiasm would make me an asset to your team.

Thank you for your time and consideration. I will call you next week to discuss setting up an interview, or you can contact me at the phone number and e-mail listed below.

Sincerely,

Tanika Ellis
21 Roosevelt Lane, Apt. 5B
Austin, TX 77016
(406) 555-6708
tanika@infonet.com

Jacob A. Sawyer
4414 St. Regis Boulevard • Miami, Florida 60024 • (617) 555-1038

March 17, 2000

Emily Meyers
Human Resources Department
Glick & Needham
51 North Shore Avenue
Miami, FL 60027

Dear Ms. Meyers,

I wanted to thank you for meeting with me today regarding the position of junior research analyst at Glick & Needham. I enjoyed the opportunity to talk with you and your staff about opportunities at your firm.

After speaking with you, I feel confident that I would be an asset to Glick & Needham. As you know, I have spent two summers working as a research analyst at J.C. Waters & Associates, where I gained valuable research, computer, and analytical skills. I also feel that my organizational skills, diligence, and problem-solving abilities make me well-suited to the position of junior research analyst.

Please feel free to call me if you have any further questions. I am very excited about the prospect of working at Glick & Needham. I will call you by March 24 to follow up.

Thank you for your time and consideration.

Sincerely,

Jacob A. Sawyer

January 21, 2000

Henry S. Liu
Vice President
Banque Royale
60 Wall Street
New York, NY 55810

Dear Mr. Liu,

Thank you for the opportunity to interview with you today for the analyst position in investment banking at Banque Royale. I very much enjoyed our discussion, and I appreciate your taking time to meet with me. I believe that investment banking is a job for which I am well qualified, and I am particularly excited about the opportunity to work at your firm.

My references have been contacted and are ready to hear from you. I look forward to speaking with you in the future.

Sincerely,

Vikram T. Bisla
114 Glen Ridge Road
Riverside, NY 32011
(581) 555-9088
vbisla@mailcom.net

NIKOLAS STAVROS
27 Sparrow Street • Philadelphia, PA 67094 • 523-555-1200

June 19, 2000

Heather Hadley
Vice President of Marketing
Westbrook Communications, Inc.
54 North Shore Boulevard
Philadelphia, PA 67090

Dear Ms. Hadley:

We met at the Highsmith College Career Fair last March and discussed my interest in marketing.

I am seeking an entry-level marketing job, preferably in the field of communications or technology. I was wondering if you might be willing to speak with me at greater length about the field in general and about your firm in particular. Hearing about your experience in marketing and detailed knowledge of the industry would be very helpful to me during my search.

I have enclosed a resume for your consideration. I will contact your office about the possibility of setting up a meeting. Or, feel free to contact me at (532) 555-1200 or nikolas.stavros@link2.net.

Many thanks for your time and help.

Sincerely,

Nikolas Stavros

February 25, 2000

Rajat Hashim
Account Manager
J&T Advertising, Inc.
616 Snowcrest Court
Lansing, MI 87114

Dear Mr. Hashim,

I wanted to thank you again for taking the time to speak with me this morning. The information you provided about the advertising industry was very helpful, and I am sure that I will utilize your advice as I continue my job search.

As we discussed, I am enclosing a resume for you to review. If you think my skills and experiences make me a good candidate for a position at J&T Advertising, please let me know.

Enjoy your vacation in Colorado. I will let you know how my job search is going from time to time.

Warmest Regards,

Maria Vasquez
PO Box 11606
Lansing, MI 87114
(788) 555-1241
vazquez@ibiz.com

January 15, 2000

Anthony Vitelli
Recruiting Administrator
Paragon Media, Inc.
55 Via del Mar, Suite 3000
Los Angeles, CA 91211

Dear Mr. Vitelli:

I wanted to thank you again for meeting with me to discuss the position of production assistant at Paragon Media, Inc. Although I was disappointed to learn the position has been filled, I still believe I have the talents and qualifications necessary to succeed at Paragon Media.

As we discussed, I have a number of qualifications that would make me an asset to your firm, including:

- A degree in communications from Western California University, where I specialized in film and television production and produced a documentary about breast cancer in low-income communities.
- Experience in film editing and production, gained during my two-year tenure as an intern at Big Cat Productions.
- Excellent leadership, organizational, and interpersonal skills, developed during four years of experience as a producer for KWCU, the Western California University radio station.

Your company's recent interest in webcasting is particularly exciting to me. I hope that you will consider me for future positions as they become available. I enclose another copy of my resume for your files. Please feel free to contact me to arrange another interview.

Thank you again for your consideration.

Sincerely,

Erin O'Connor
7 Perry Drive
Los Angeles, CA 91230
(982) 555-3911
eoconnor@spellnet.org

Annabel J. Darden
Strathmore & Beckett
255 West Delancy Avenue
San Diego, CA 94820
(914) 555-1000

June 10, 2000

Dear Friends,

I wanted to let you all know that I have accepted a paralegal position at the law firm of Strathmore & Beckett,
based in San Diego. Strathmore & Beckett is an entertainment law firm, where I will be working with a wide variety
of clients from the publishing, broadcasting, and music
industries. I have received a warm welcome from the S&B
team, and I am very much looking forward to the challenges
and opportunities that this job will provide.

Many thanks for all of the support and guidance that you
gave me during my job search. Without the invaluable help
of my friends and acquaintances, I might not have found a
job so well suited to my strengths and interests.

My new e-mail address is adarden@strathbeck.com, and I can
be reached by phone at (914) 555-1000, extension 388.

I hope this letter finds you well, and I look forward to
hearing from you soon.

Best Wishes,

Annabel

A P P E N D I X E

sample package 1

Robert DiNapoli

Robert's Cover Letter

Robert's Resume

Robert's Thank-You Letter

ROBERT DiNAPOLI

78 Glen Rd., Kent, KY 52039   E-mail: dinapoli@netlink.com   Phone: (413) 456-7890

April 13, 2000

Ms. Isabel Plum
Human Resources Manager
Bloomington's Department Store
1000 Mockingbird Avenue
Louisville, KY 53092

Dear Ms. Plum:

I am answering your ad in the *Louisville Gazette* for the assistant buyer position in the Men's Department of Bloomington's Department Store.

I am a recent graduate of Westbrook Academy, where I majored in merchandising and design with a minor in French. My work experience has been in a variety of menswear boutiques; I have had both customer service and assistant buying responsibilities.

Currently, I'm managing a staff of 11 sales associates. However, I have made the career decision to find a position that will help me attain my goal of becoming a menswear buyer.

Due to my academic and work experience, I feel that I am uniquely qualified for the assistant buyer position. I will be contacting you within the next several days to set up an appointment.

Thank you in advance for your consideration.

Sincerely,

Robert DiNapoli

ROBERT DiNAPOLI

78 Glen Rd., Kent, KY 52039   E-mail: dinapoli@netlink.com   Phone: (413) 456-7890

EDUCATION

Westbrook Academy of Design, Louisville, KY
- Associate's Degree in Merchandising and Design
- Honors: Dean's List, C. Hartley Design Award

EXPERIENCE

Franklin Beane Clotherie, Louisville, KY   1999 to present
Assistant Manager
Responsible for inventory and sales tracking management. Supervised 11 sales associates.
- Planned and implemented an automated inventory tracking system, improving store sell-through over the last two quarters.
- Created the successful "Super Tuesday" promotion, resulting in a 30% increase in Tuesday sales in the last quarter.

R&M Murphy, Hadleyville, KY   1996–1998
Salesperson
Responsible for managing the retail operations of the Men's Department, including supervising and scheduling staff, tallying receipts, providing customer service, and serving as a liaison between buying office and the sales floor.
- Developed a VIP customer tracking and notification system which increased customer purchases 25% during special sale periods.
- Received "Employee of the Month" award four times.

Peterson Clothing, Inc., Louisville, KY   1995
Intern
Responsible for analyzing buying trends and maintaining a database of retail markets for stores in Kentucky and Ohio.
- Developed a database of retail markets utilizing Microsoft Access and other computer programs
- Researched retail sales, pricing, and buying trends in Kentucky and Ohio; generated monthly reports, providing retail information to four offices.

COMMUNITY SERVICE AND ACTIVITIES

Westbrook Committee on Student Affairs, Vice President
Big Brothers/Big Sisters Program, Volunteer
Louisville Men's Soccer League

LANGUAGES

Fluent in French

REFERENCES AVAILABLE UPON REQUEST

ROBERT DiNAPOLI

78 Glen Rd., Kent, KY 52039   E-mail: dinapoli@netlink.com   Phone: (413) 456-7890

April 14, 2000

Ms. Isabel Plum
Human Resources Manager
Bloomington's Department Store
1000 Mockingbird Avenue
Louisville, KY 53092

Dear Ms. Plum:

Thank you for taking the time to meet with me yesterday. I am confident that my research experience in sales, pricing, and buying trends makes me a good match for the assistant buyer position at Bloomington's Department Store.

As we discussed, I will call you to follow up if I do not hear from you within the next week. I look forward to speaking with you soon.

Sincerely,

Robert DiNapoli

A P P E N D I X F

sample package 2

Ramona Lewis

Ramona's Cover Letter

Ramona's Resume

Ramona's Thank-You Letter

Ramona's Reconsideration Letter

RAMONA LEWIS

• 555 Cinquento Way, New York, NY 51933   •   (212) 555-6322   •   ramona@five.com

April 14, 2000

Ms. Julia Johnson
Human Resources Recruiter
Worldwide Media
777 Universe Drive
New York, NY 55555

Dear Ms. Johnson:

Jim Allen, your former colleague at Worldwide Media and a current editor at Leroux Publishing, suggested that I write to you. I worked for Jim last summer as a marketing assistant. His firm is not currently hiring, but he believed I might be a good candidate for a marketing position at Worldwide Media.

I am an excellent researcher, with additional experience in analyzing market data, planning special events, and managing staff. I have also gained valuable leadership experiences as group leader for my college chapter of Amnesty International and as coordinator of the Willard Community Players. In addition, I have some international experience: I spent a semester studying and working in Ireland.

Through my research, I know that your firm publishes the best-rated magazine for European travel, and I look forward to hearing more about your company. I've enclosed a copy of my resume and will contact you within the next several days to set up an appointment.

Sincerely,

Ramona Lewis

RAMONA LEWIS

- 555 Cinquento Way, New York, NY 51933 • (212) 555-6322 • ramona@five.com

EDUCATION

Willard University, St. Louis, MO
Bachelor of Arts, Business; GPA: 3.81

University College Dublin, Dublin, Ireland
Spring, 1997; Coursework in finance and marketing.

EXPERIENCE

Leroux Publishing, St. Louis, MO   May 1999–Aug. 1999
Marketing Assistant
Responsible for competitive and consumer market research for the Midwest region.
- Generated critical weekly reports on the demographics, purchasing, and education patterns of the 18–25 year old market segment.
- Created and maintained database of consumer and competitor information for five departments, improving efficiency of marketing department.

Willard Business Library, St. Louis, MO   Jan. 1996–Dec. 1998
Library Assistant
Responsible for circulation desk management along with computerized book rental and inventory system.
- Managed circulation desk.
- Operated computerized book rental and inventory system.

Video Bonanza, Branson, MO   Sept. 1994–Aug. 1995
Sales Clerk
Responsible for customer service, cash register operation and Saturday store opening procedure.
- Managed courtesy desk, handling an average of 45 customer transactions per day; resolved customer complaints.
- Prepared Saturday bank deposits and reconciled receipts with 100% accuracy.

**COMMUNITY
LEADERSHIP**

Amnesty International   Jan. 1998–Jan. 1999
Group Leader
Responsible for organizing events to raise campus and community awareness of local and international human rights issues.
- Led weekly meetings and membership drives, leading to a 25% increase in membership.
- Developed Speakers Bureau and invited human rights advocates and government officials to discuss their views on campus, resulting in coverage on two major television networks.

Willard Community Players   Jan. 1997–June 1999
Coordinator
Head of a theater group that performs plays and musicals to raise money for nonprofit organizations.
- Planned fundraiser that resulted in a 50% increase in ticket sales.
- Performed in *What's for Dinner?* and *Grease.*

SKILLS

Microsoft Office, WordPerfect, Power Point, HTML

RAMONA LEWIS

- 555 Cinquento Way, New York, NY 51933   •   (212) 555-6322   •   ramona@five.com

April 20, 2000

Ms. Julia Johnson
Human Resources Recruiter
Worldwide Media
777 Universe Drive
New York, NY 55555

Dear Ms. Johnson:

Thank you for taking the time to meet with me yesterday. I enjoyed the opportunity to learn about the job of marketing coordinator.

I am very enthusiastic about the position at Worldwide Media, and I am particularly excited about the prospect of studying the viability of a new travel magazine focusing on Ireland. I believe that my experiences living in Dublin and traveling throughout Ireland give me a unique perspective on the attractiveness of the country as a destination for college students.

Please do not hesitate to contact me by phone or e-mail if you need anything further. I will contact you next week to discuss the next steps.

Sincerely,

Ramona Lewis

RAMONA LEWIS

- 555 Cinquento Way, New York, NY 51933 • (212) 555-6322 • ramona@five.com

April 24, 2000

Ms. Julia Johnson
Human Resources Recruiter
Worldwide Media
777 Universe Drive
New York, NY 55555

Dear Ms. Johnson:

Thank you for taking the time to meet with me on Monday. While I was disappointed to hear that I was declined for the position of marketing coordinator, I very much enjoyed having the opportunity to learn about the position and your company.

My interest in the field of marketing and in your company remains, and I hope that you will consider me in the future as positions become available. I would appreciate the opportunity to come in for another interview at your convenience, and can be reached at the same number and address.

Thank you for your time and consideration.

Sincerely,

Ramona Lewis

Sample Case Interviews

Estimation Cases

Business Cases

PRACTICE CASE 1: ESTIMATION CASE

PROBLEM: How many pieces of luggage do you think are unloaded at LaGuardia Airport each day?

In this type of case, your job is to work through a series of estimations to produce a numerical answer to the question. As the interview goes on, you will need to interact with your interviewer, obtain information, and check your thinking. Explain your logic at each stage of the problem, and ask your interviewer whether your assumptions are correct. In all likelihood, your interviewer won't provide you with the hard numbers you need for intermediate steps, but ask you to make a few assumptions and come up with them yourself.

As you work through the problem, think carefully about what assumptions you are making, and the ways in which they could be wrong. It doesn't matter if your answer is right, as long as you have thought about it logically, and recognized the parts of your solution that you could change to generate the correct answer.

The interview could sound something like this:

Interviewer: Why don't you tell me how many pieces of luggage you think are unloaded at LaGuardia Airport each day.

Candidate: Okay, let me ask a few clarifying questions first. When you say, "unloaded," do you mean baggage that is just handled or that people actually pick up?

I: That people pick up at the baggage claim.

C: Okay. Well, I think we should figure out how many people fly in to LaGuardia each day, and how many bags they carry. A good starting point is probably to figure out how many flights arrive. Now, LaGuardia is mostly a domestic airport, right?

I: Right.

C: Let's assume, then, that there are two kinds of airlines that use the airport. Major carriers that use the airport as a hub will have more flights arriving than those that do not.

I: Sounds fair. So how many major carriers do you think use LaGuardia?

C: Well, let's see. There's Delta, American, United, USAir . . . why don't we say four major carriers, and ten smaller airlines. Figure that the larger carriers have ten flights arriving per hour, between the hours of 8 A.M. and midnight. Does that sound correct?

I: 8 A.M. may be a little early for flights to arrive . . . that means they would have to leave at around 6 A.M., and there aren't too many of those.

C: Okay, let's say 9 A.M. to midnight. That gives us 150 flights per major carrier per day, times 4 major carriers, gives us 600 arriving flights per day . . .

... and so on. The basic strategy, though, is the same for the whole problem. Ultimately, you need three facts: (1) the number of flights per day; (2) the number of passengers per flight; (3) the number of bags per passenger.

Once you have the number of flights, there are several factors that you may want to consider to compute the number of passengers per flight: percentage of passengers, by carrier type, for whom New York is the final destination (i.e. passengers who would pick up their luggage at LaGuardia); average capacity per flight; and the average percentage of seats sold per flight. Taking into account both major and minor carriers, you would arrive at an estimate of the number of passengers deplaning at LGA.

The final step is to compute the number of bags per passenger. Here it might be useful to distinguish between passengers traveling for business and for pleasure, because business passengers tend to check fewer bags. Once you have the approximate number of business and personal travelers for each type of carrier, estimate the number of bags you think each type of passenger carries. Then use your number to calculate the total number of bags passing through LaGuardia each day, based on your earlier estimates and assumptions.

The key to estimation cases is in recognizing that each piece of the puzzle must be divided into its parts, and that each part must be analyzed separately.

The conclusion of the estimate interview is supposed to be a number, so keep that in mind as you are driving toward the answer, and be sure to take good notes so that you can add it all up in the end.

PRACTICE CASE 2: BUSINESS CASE

PROBLEM: Imagine that you are a consultant, hired by Carnegie Hall, a large concert hall in New York City. For the past several years, their profits have been declining, and they want you to figure out how to reverse this trend and restore profitability.

Business cases tend to be more structured than estimation cases. The interview will be an interactive conversation in which your interviewer will answer your queries, ask you some questions, and provide guidance as you solve the problem.

Most case interviews proceed similarly. Your interviewer first sets up the problem. Sometimes, the interviewer will introduce the problem very specifically and narrowly, so that your task is clear. Other times, the case will be more open-ended, and it will be up to you to introduce greater structure.

From there, you should follow four basic steps: clarify, structure, analyze, and conclude. Take a few minutes at first to ask some clarifying questions, or restate the problem in your own words, to make sure that you understand it well. When you are clear about what you are being asked to do, move on.

Perhaps the most important step is structuring the problem. Think about what the major components of the analysis should be. For instance, if the question asks about profitability, the major components would be revenues and costs. Or, alternatively, think about the series of questions that you have to answer in order to make a recommendation. If the case is about entering a new market, some of the questions that you would have to answer to make that decision include what the company's capabilities are, how lucrative the market is, and what the competitive landscape is like. In any event, the idea is to organize your thoughts—then you can dive in and analyze each major category.

As you conduct your analysis, keep in mind whether the information you are receiving and the conclusions that you are drawing really answer the question. Try to think about *what information you will need* and ask your interviewer questions to get that information. If you are trying to increase profitability, and have found out that to do so, you must increase the quantity of goods sold, brainstorm ways that you can do this, and run your ideas by your interviewer.

Finally, at the end of the interview, take a minute to summarize the analysis you have conducted and the conclusions that you have drawn.

The steps below describe one possible answer to this case. *There are many possible answers!* The important thing is to keep a logical structure in your head as you go through the case. Keep your thoughts in order, and think carefully about what information you need, or what questions you should be asking next.

Let's run through each step of the analysis:

1. Since this is a profitability question, our hypothetical consultant has broken the issue down into two parts: revenues and costs (Profit = Revenue - Cost). He decides to start with revenues, and asks his interviewer whether they have been declining. The interviewer says yes.

2. There are many possible sources of revenues for Carnegie Hall, such as advertising, donations, and ticket sales, so our consultant lists a number of possibilities and runs them by his interviewer. She says that most have remained steady for the past six months, except for ticket sales, which have declined.

3. Knowing that ticket sales are declining, the consultant determines that there can be two causes for this decline. Carnegie Hall is either failing to attract audiences, or lowering its price. Our consultant begins with audiences, and asks the interviewer if box office sales have been declining. It turns out that they are.

4. Our consultant pushes this a little, trying to figure out which people are no longer coming to Carnegie Hall. He asks about age groups, and is told that there has been a decline across the board. He then asks about what kind of music people have been coming to hear. The interviewer tells him that classical music makes up the bulk of Carnegie Hall sales.

5. Our consultant assumes that younger audiences favor rock music, and that older audiences favor classical. The interviewer agrees. So, one reason why younger people are no longer coming could be the lack of rock music. But that still doesn't explain why older people aren't turning out. He

asks about the competition . . . specifically, what mix of shows Carnegie Hall's competitors are showing. Radio City Music Hall, the closest competitor shows many more rock shows than Carnegie Hall—explaining, the consultant surmises, the decline in our market share among youth. Radio City shows a lower percentage of classical shows, but the same number of shows overall. So why are audiences going there?

6. Thinking that there is another factor at play here, the consultant shifts to talking about price, and quickly finds out from his interviewer that Carnegie Hall charges 30% more for tickets than Radio City. No wonder the classical audiences go there—same number of shows, but they cost less. How can this be?

7. Staying with price, our consultant asks about the ticket prices for rock shows. Here, Radio City is able to charge a 50% premium since younger audiences are willing to pay more to see their favorite stars. This means, he surmises, that they can afford to charge less for the classical shows.

8. Summing up, it looks like there are several options for Carnegie Hall to increase its revenues, and therefore (assuming costs stay constant) its profits:
   - It can introduce rock shows and use the ticket premiums to subsidize classical music
   - It can increase the frequency of shows at a lower price
   - It can engage in a marketing campaign to promote classical music and draw younger audiences willing to pay their prices.

This practice case is somewhat simplified, but gets to most of the major issues. In reality, costs would be a factor, especially in the second recommendation above, and a good interviewer would likely want you to address that. But this should serve as a basic model of the thought process that goes into cases. The additional examples below will provide you with some extra practice.

PRACTICE MAKES PERFECT

Here are some examples of both estimation questions and full cases. It is best to work on these with friends, though it will also be helpful to just think about it yourself, and try to sketch out an issue tree describing how you would break down and analyze each case.

Estimation questions

- Estimate the number of McDonald's restaurants in the world.
- What is the total amount of money lost by the Postal Service because of e-mail?
- What is the approximate size of the U.S. market for compact discs?

Business case questions

- The Chicago Cubs are interested in building a new baseball stadium, and are trying to decide if they should do it. Things to consider in the decision include the demand and supply for baseball tickets (in a two-team market), the capital investment in the stadium and expected return (in all likelihood, you would only deal with these concepts if you know something about finance), and the strategic rationale for a new stadium.
- A major U.S. pharmaceutical company is trying to decide whether to open an overseas branch, and contracts you to perform some feasibility analysis for them.

I N D E X

Get Noticed,
Get Hired

Create the perfect resume package—
cover letters that get read and
resumes that get results

Prepare your resume so it scans
without glitches

Design a web-friendly resume for
electronic submission

by Jason R. Rich

WHAT DOES YOUR RESUME *REALLY* SAY ABOUT YOU?

GREAT RESUME

Create a resume that gets the right response

The very first impression you make when you're job seeking isn't the one you impart when you shake hands, it's the impression you make when you submit your resume. Learn how to analyze your strengths and "sell yourself" effectively.

GREAT RESUME will help you get in the door – and into the job you want. It provides you with valuable information such as:

- **How to select the right resume format for your situation**
- **What are the key questions your resume must answer**
- **How to make sure your resume scans properly**
- **How to create web-friendly resumes for electronic submission**
- **What to include with your resume**
- **How to avoid the Top 25 resume mistakes**
- **The best words to incorporate in a cover letter**